SOAR to
Business Success

SOAR to Business Success

Creating Sustainable Growth and Value

Larry Goddard, Laurence Franklin, and Jennifer Goddard

Published by Game Changer Publishing

Cover Design: Skylar Ringenbach

Paperback ISBN: 978-1-966659-25-9

Hardcover ISBN: 978-1-966659-26-6

Digital ISBN: 978-1-966659-27-3

GC | GAME CHANGER PUBLISHING

www.GameChangerPublishing.com

Dedication

To past and present clients, team members, and partners who helped us shape the SOAR methodology and process—our heartfelt gratitude. Your expertise, collaboration, and passion built a lasting foundation that continues to inspire growth in our every endeavor.

To the future SOAR community, we salute your courage in exploring new frontiers, and your willingness to embrace new perspectives. May your commitment light the way for continued growth, innovation, progress, and discovery.

Thank You for Wanting to SOAR

Just to say thanks we would like to give you a free SOARgrowth consultation, no strings attached!

Scan the QR Code Here:

SOAR to Business Success

*Creating Sustainable
Growth and Value*

**Larry Goddard,
Laurence Franklin,
and
Jennifer Goddard**

Table of Contents

Chapter 1: Nurturing the Spark to SOAR 11

Chapter 2: Importance of Growth 21

Chapter 3: Our Growth Journey 25

Chapter 4: Introduction to SOAR 29

Chapter 5: Painting Your Business's Growth Picture 31

Chapter 6: The SOAR Growth Engine 37

Chapter 7: Turning Hypothesis into Reality 49

Chapter 8: Sales Execution 53

Chapter 9: Good Days Lead to Sales Success and Growth 59

Chapter 10: Value Proposition and Elevator Pitch 63

Chapter 11: Margin Growth 69

Chapter 12: Organization and Culture 75

Chapter 13: Buy-In 81

Chapter 14: Leadership 87

Chapter 15: Power of Teamwork 91

Chapter 16: Accounting, Finance, and Technology 95

Chapter 17: Responsiveness and Execution 105

Chapter 18: Pivoting 115

Chapter 19: Time to SOAR! 119

Our Companion to SOAR: SOARgrowth 123

About the Authors 125

Chapter 1
Nurturing the Spark to SOAR

We've spent our careers chasing one thing: growth. Whether it was helping businesses find their footing or taking them to unimaginable heights, we've been in the trenches, as leaders or side by side with them, navigating challenges and uncovering opportunities. Collectively, the three of us have over a century of combined experience—not just years on paper, but real-world lessons learned through trial, error, and success.

When we talk about growth, we don't just mean increasing sales (though, let's be honest, that's usually high on the wish list). Growth is about creating a ripple effect—boosting productivity, building efficiency, nurturing creativity, and unlocking the full potential of your business in ways that leave a lasting impact. It's about profitability, yes, but also about building a culture, fostering knowledge, and tapping into the kind of innovation that sets you apart.

Over the years, we've developed growth strategies that don't just live in theory—they've been validated in real life with hundreds of businesses, big and small. And through it all, we've come to embrace two universal truths about growth:

1. Most businesses have the potential to grow—if they have the appropriate vision, creativity, flexibility and resources.

2. Proven methodologies, tools, and approaches can significantly enhance the chances for success.

In this book, we'll share the tools, insights, and strategies we've fine-tuned over decades to help businesses thrive. Think of it as a roadmap—one that meets you where you are and helps you chart the steps your business can take toward the growth you desire.

According to the U.S. Chamber of Commerce, 99.9% of businesses in the United States are small and medium-sized businesses (with under five hundred employees), and their biggest obstacle is their ability to grow.

The good news is that most businesses have the potential to grow significantly and create lasting value if they have access to the appropriate tools, methodologies, and resources. A significant proportion of U.S. companies reach revenue of between $1 million and $5 million, and a further portion achieves even greater sales volumes, with many approaching $100 million or more. Growth is there for your business to attain: growth in revenues, earnings, value, reputation, resilience, and longevity.

This book provides you with proven strategies to take the wheel and steer your business toward growth and value creation. You will become well-versed and equipped with the same tools, insights, and guidance that have delivered transformative results for our companies, our clients, and many of the highest-growth businesses in the U.S. and around the world.

The possibilities are yours to discover. Business growth is well within your reach, so let's get going and SOAR!

Requirements for Growth

The basis for business success and growth is to establish the appropriate:

1. Passion
2. Plan
3. Talent
4. Resources

The only item you absolutely need to begin is the first: passion.

With the right amount of passion and the determination this brings, you will likely be able to develop and build the right plan, talent, and resources. This applies to existing businesses that want to grow and to start-ups.

"Passion" is the critical starting point and:

- Is the core of being an entrepreneur and business leader.
- Is the foundation of the business leader's intensity, enthusiasm, commitment, and drive.
- Is the essence that fuels a creative vision and compelling mission. It sustains the emotional energy, dedication to the business, and drive to pursue goals, overcome challenges, and continually seek innovation, improvement, and growth.
- Fuels perseverance and resilience.

- Attracts talent and investors and enhances customer relationships, company culture, and long-term growth potential.
- Makes the entrepreneurial journey more fulfilling. While entrepreneurship involves hard work and sacrifices, passionate entrepreneurs find joy in the process itself, not just in the outcomes. This sense of fulfillment can be a key driver for long-term sustainability and well-being.

Unmet Need

Passion invariably starts with an idea—about a product or service that is needed or desired by existing or potential customers. Business founders believe that this need or desire is not currently being adequately fulfilled in the marketplace and, therefore, there is an opportunity to fill the unmet need.

Identifying this "unmet need"—together with the passion to pursue it—is the spark that ignites the growth process. An entrepreneur with a great idea and passion can usually develop the plan, talent, and resources to turn the idea into reality.

Here are several well-known examples of entrepreneurs who identified unmet needs in the marketplace and successfully developed businesses to capitalize on them:

1. **Steve Jobs and Steve Wozniak—Apple**

   Personal computing for the masses. In the 1970s, computers were mainly used by large companies, universities, and government organizations. An affordable, user-friendly computer for personal use was a rarity. Apple created a lot of attention, but it was actually many years before they became market leaders. Their passion provided the spark, but they went through several iterations of plans, people, products, and financial ups and downs before they evolved into what they are today.

2. **Reed Hastings—Netflix**

   Convenient and affordable access to movies. In the late 1990s, renting movies required visiting physical stores (such as Blockbuster) that charged rental fees and additional fees for late returns. There was a need for more convenient and cost-effective movie rental options. Netflix began life offering at-home convenience and assortment via the mail, and then, as technology evolved, it transitioned to a streaming platform, disrupting the entertainment industry.

3. **Jeff Bezos—Amazon**

   From online bookstore to global marketplace and cloud computing. What started as a convenient and reliable way to buy books online has now become the largest marketplace in the world. In the early 1990s, people had limited options for purchasing books, especially if they lived in areas without large bookstores. Bezos identified the Internet as a revolutionary platform for e-commerce. He started Amazon as an online bookstore that provided a much wider selection of titles than brick-and-mortar stores. Amazon used data to personalize recommendations and create an intuitive shopping experience. Bezos's ability to identify unmet consumer needs (speed, convenience, and variety) and continually innovate propelled Amazon's growth and opened the doors to other business opportunities, such as cloud computing services. Amazon's AWS is now the market leader for cloud computing and hosting.

4. **Brian Chesky, Joe Gebbia, and Nathan Blecharczyk—Airbnb**

   Affordable and unique lodging options. Who would have believed that staying in a room in a stranger's apartment would be a turn-on for millions of travelers? Airbnb disrupted the hospitality industry by creating a massive peer-to-peer rental marketplace that blended cost-effective lodging with the ability to experience local customs, food, and culture. It is now a multi-billion-dollar company with millions of listings in cities around the world.

Most of the above examples of unmet needs involved new and revolutionary products or ways to deliver them. Here are some examples of ideas that filled unmet needs by focusing on service, quality, cost-effectiveness, and ease of doing business:

1. **Zappos—Customer Service Excellence**

   A superior online shopping experience with exceptional customer service. Before Zappos, online retailers often focused on product selection and pricing, but customer service was neglected, leading to customer frustration, returns, and exchanges. Zappos became known for its "customer-obsessed" culture and set new standards for customer service in e-commerce, showing that improving customer experience can be a key to business success without a revolutionary product.

2. **IKEA—Affordable, Self-Assembled Furniture**

   Affordable, modern furniture for budget-conscious consumers. Traditionally, well-designed furniture was both expensive and often required costly delivery and assembly services. IKEA offered affordable, flat-pack furniture that customers could transport and assemble themselves, significantly reducing costs—and also offered delivery and assembly if desired by the customer. Their model made design-forward furniture accessible to a wider audience. IKEA became a global leader in the furniture market by addressing the unmet need for stylish, budget-friendly furniture, using an innovative business model rather than a revolutionary product.

3. **Dollar Shave Club—Subscription-Based Razors**

   Affordable and convenient razors. Before Dollar Shave Club, buying razors involved paying for brand-name razors and their expensive replacement blades. Additionally, the experience of purchasing razors in-store was often inconvenient. Dollar Shave Club offered a subscription-based service that delivered razors and shaving products directly to customers' homes at a low monthly cost. The business eliminated the inconvenience and high cost associated with traditional razor purchases.

These examples involved three important business success factors: innovation, resilience, and openness to change. These companies differentiated themselves from the competition, persevered through difficult times, and adapted based on their learning and experience to remain relevant in a changing world.

But you don't always have to come up with a unique, earth-shattering idea. There are many ways to serve the needs of current or potential customers. These include:

1. Finding opportunities to outperform your competitors—to obtain a larger market share.
2. Providing existing products and services in underserved geographic areas.
3. Expanding offerings (new colors, sizes, styles, flavors, features, benefits) in ways that will expand your audience and improve the chances they will pick you for the product or service.

Very few highly successful entrepreneurs—at the time they develop their idea of the unmet need—have the detailed plans, talent, and resources to generate the growth they ultimately achieve. However, rest assured, they have the passion to marshal them.

Don't Underestimate the Power of Your Passion

Whether you are looking at starting a business venture or you already have an established company, bringing to life the ideas that will fuel progress can be a difficult process. Often, the idea is simple—it is the execution that is challenging. This is where your passion and spark make a key difference. Don't let a good idea languish because you feel you do not have the right plan, talent, or resources to "make it happen."

Holding off on pursuing an opportunity is one of the biggest impediments to both initial and ongoing successes. Please know that virtually every entrepreneur or business leader starts in this position.

If you have an idea and enough passion, it is not essential to have all the talent and resources available to explore making that idea a reality. Confident and experienced entrepreneurs know that what is lacking can be "acquired" or "sourced." They are able to temporarily "suspend disbelief" and allow the opportunity to evolve on the assumption that the missing pieces will be filled in. They focus on the outcome—decide if it is worthwhile, and then they work on how to bring the idea to life.

With the right amount of passion and the determination this brings, you will likely be able to develop and build the right plan, talent, and resources.

There are consultants, advisors, mentors, coaches, business incubators, lenders, and investors who can assist in getting the idea off the ground and identifying where and how to obtain the appropriate talent and resources.

Later in the book, we will discuss in more detail the topics of funding your business for growth and maximizing your working capital.

We Are Here for All of You

While only a rare few individual entrepreneurs have been able to generate an initial "spark" that turns into giant, global businesses, there have been many thousands of successful entrepreneurs who have, in their own unique way, created millions of local, regional, and national businesses that drive the U.S. and world economy.

We salute those who have the spark and passion to take risks and work hard for the rewards. We know that it takes perseverance, intuition, skill, and sometimes good fortune to turn passion into reality and stay the course. This is your moment to SOAR—to break past barriers, realize your dreams, and build a legacy of growth and success. Let's take the next step together. The future you envision is waiting, and we're here to help you make it a reality.

This book is for all of you who have that entrepreneurial spirit. We understand the risks you take, the challenges you face, and the rewards you work so hard to earn. That is why we developed the SOAR methodology and process and also its powerful companion app, SOARgrowth (www.SOARgrowth.com).

For Established and Start-Up Businesses

This book is designed for business leaders seeking to improve their results. Whether you are an established business experiencing slow or stalled growth or believe that your business has more potential than it is demonstrating, the SOAR process and philosophy for attaining growth can offer benefits. You will find actionable strategies and proven methodologies to help you explore the growth opportunities available to your business.

At the same time, the principles and frameworks presented here are equally valuable for start-ups. Building a strong foundation early in a company's lifecycle is critical to long-term success. The SOAR tools and practices will help you identify growth opportunities, avoid common pitfalls, and create scalable systems that support your vision.

Conclusion

Every great business begins with a spark—a combination of passion, purpose, and the belief that there is a better way to serve your customers, solve a problem, or meet an unmet need. This spark is the driving force behind growth, innovation, and lasting success. Whether you are looking to reignite growth in an established business or build a start-up from the ground up, the SOAR methodology provides the framework to transform your ideas into actionable strategies and your passion into sustainable results.

Growth is not a linear or assured journey, and challenges are inevitable. However, with the right plan, talent, and resources—and unwavering determination fueled by your passion—you have the power to confront obstacles and explore new opportunities. The SOAR program is here to guide your every step—to stimulate you to harness your spark, chart a clear course, and equip you with the tools to pursue growth. Now is the time to take the leap and set your business on the path to SOAR. Let's begin the journey.

—

Chapter 2
Importance of Growth

Growth is the lifeblood of a business. It is the driving force that propels a business forward.

Growing businesses have an energy that motivates team members, entices customers, threatens competitors, attracts suppliers, and rewards owners.

- *Growth creates the potential to enhance wealth.* Bigger businesses frequently generate more profitability, cash flow, and value.

- *Growth is attractive* to current and potential employees, who see more advancement opportunities; to customers, who like to be associated with a winner; and to financial institutions and investors, who see the potential for positive returns with less risk.

- *Growth can make a business more competitive.* With improved revenues and profitability, businesses have the choice of how best to invest. Expanded buying power can result in lower costs; larger volumes can generate operational efficiency via economies of scale and automation; enhanced resources facilitate greater investment in R&D and marketing, which can improve the value proposition and expand brand recognition.

- *Growth creates momentum,* which, when managed properly, can sustain positive market share gains and propel the company toward long-term success.

The desire to maintain growth can be the catalyst that pushes the company to remain innovative, engaged, and competitive.

However, there are risks to growth:

- *Growth can stretch a company's resources.* Without control and discipline, growth can throw the business's finances, manpower, supply chain, quality, and customer resources off balance.

- *Growth frequently involves developing and tackling new strategic initiatives,* many of which could have steep learning curves, like new products, customers, territories and channels.

- *Growth can stretch company leaders beyond their capabilities.* Entering new and uncharted territory in terms of size, scale, products, and services may require an evolution of the management team. Knowing how to deal with what the business doesn't know and needs to put into place is often what separates companies that achieve lasting success from the ones that sputter or fail.

- *Growth can distract and defocus.* With attention and energy directed to the new activities, there is potential for neglect of the core business operations that successfully brought the business to its current state.

- *Growth can be stressful.* While there is more upside to a growing business, more things can go wrong, creating worry and stress for its leaders.

- *Growth frequently incorporates financial risks and tradeoffs,* which can include additional debt, personal guarantees for debt, and ownership dilution.

- *Growth can cause businesses to become overconfident or complacent,* where businesses lose the edge that fueled their growth. Staying disciplined, focused, and forward-thinking is essential to ensuring growth is not just a phase but a foundation for enduring success.

As business owners, executives, and advisors, we have helped develop and implement turnaround and growth strategies for hundreds of businesses. Based on this experience, we believe that the benefits of pursuing business growth are worth the risks in most situations. Growth is not for the faint of heart and is a decision every business leader must make for themselves.

We have experienced both the rewards of growth and the risks associated with executing a growth plan. We have a healthy respect for the challenges presented by changing the culture, the business dynamics, and, at times, the financial leverage of the business. Being an entrepreneur who is committed to the pursuit of growth requires fortitude, resilience, and confidence. Dealing with the ups and downs and stresses and strains that will invariably occur takes a toll. Having a supportive and balanced home life and a good team around the business is a great help in this area.

Growing businesses have an energy that motivates team members, entices customers, threatens competitors, attracts suppliers, and rewards owners.

Controlled Growth

Because of the risks of growth, we advocate for "controlled growth," which encompasses:

1. *Pursuing strategic initiatives that have a greater chance of short-term and long-term success.* Focus on the opportunities and necessities that, in terms of cost, timeframe, and degree of difficulty to develop, test, and implement, fit the company's capabilities, resources, and bandwidth. This does not mean you don't consider high-impact (and potentially high-risk) initiatives. It means you manage the risk and put in place the necessary ingredients to execute the plan successfully.

2. *Steering towards "downhill rides."* These are strategic initiatives that encompass:

   a. Markets where demand for the products or services is strong and growing.

   b. Attractive margins.

   c. Less entrenched and dominant competitors.

   d. Less customer concentration (markets with a few large and dominant customers—like Amazon, Walmart, or the U.S. military—create an imbalance of power toward the customer)

3. *Planning carefully and diligently.* This includes:

   a. A clear and documented understanding of the Current State of the business and the desired Future State (aka "vision").

   b. Details of how the business will advance from the Current State to the Future State.

   c. Comprehensive financial and cash flow budgets and projections.

   d. Extensive capacity planning, including talent, manpower, equipment, buildings, supply chain, and inventory.

4. *Realistic progress assessments and pivots.* These incorporate:

   a. Regular evaluation of actual progress and results compared to plans, budgets, and projections.

   b. A diligent and honest evaluation of the extent of and reasons for variations from plans, budgets, and projections.

   c. Constant updating of the plans, budgets, and projections to fit evolving internal and external conditions and developments.

Conclusion

Growth is an important driver of progress, innovation, and success in any business. While it presents risks, challenges, and stress, the rewards of growth—enhanced financial resources, competitiveness, and momentum—frequently make it a worthwhile pursuit for those with the vision and determination to navigate its complexities. Growth requires discipline, planning, and a commitment to balancing opportunity with risk.

By embracing the concept of "controlled growth," businesses can help mitigate risks while seizing opportunities. This involves selecting strategic initiatives that align with the company's capabilities and resources, planning meticulously for transitions, and remaining agile in the face of evolving circumstances. Controlled growth is not about avoiding challenges but managing them effectively. Businesses that control growth can achieve sustainable progress without compromising their core operations or long-term vision.

The pursuit of growth is not for the faint of heart. However, resilience, fortitude, and a dedicated team can lead to remarkable success. Growth requires courage, but it also provides the energy and momentum that propel businesses forward. When approached with careful planning and a commitment to adaptability, growth can facilitate not just an aspiration but a lasting legacy of achievement.

Chapter 3
Our Growth Journey

Our careers have been devoted to the relentless pursuit of business growth.

As owners, executives, consultants, advisors, and board members, we have helped develop and implement growth strategies for hundreds of businesses. Using the SOAR principles, we have collectively contributed to the creation of billions in public and private business value.

Here are just a few accomplishments that we are particularly proud of:

Laurence was the vice president and then president and CEO of Tumi. Over 18 years, he led Tumi from a small company doing under $4 million per year in revenues to a leading global brand, generating annual sales of over $450 million. He was also the president of Coach, the leather goods and accessories brand. Under his leadership, Coach more than doubled sales to over $500 million and tripled earnings. Laurence was a board member and advisor at Rosetta Stone, a leading language learning and education technology business. During his time there, sales grew eightfold, and the business executed a successful IPO and then, several years later, an even more successful "take private" sale.

Larry was the CEO of a construction equipment company for eight years, where he led the business from $3 million in sales to $100 million. Larry was also CEO of a metal products company, where profits grew almost tenfold in less than 2 years. He became an advisor to a distributor of construction products that grew its sales from $50 million to close to $200 million, and a manufacturer of military products that grew from $4 million to over $100 million, both of which saw corresponding increases in profitability.

Jennifer was the Chief of Sales and Marketing for a national manufacturing company. Over a three-year period, she led the sales team to more than double the revenue at significantly enhanced margins. As a national sales manager of a consumer products manufacturer, she developed a channel strategy that displaced the products of a Fortune 500 company, facilitating tenfold growth in several national retailers. In addition, Jennifer recruited a national sales force of 84 people for a novelty and giftware company, driving an 85% sales increase in less than six months.

In all these situations, growth was sparked by the identification of unmet needs, outperforming the competition, or both.

Early in our management careers, we were struck with the realization that it was difficult for small and medium-sized businesses to achieve and sustain growth versus larger competitors. Smaller businesses lacked the resources to access appropriate tools, techniques, mentors, and professional relationships. In our case, we had the benefit of post-graduate business degrees and certifications from leading schools and organizations. We read business articles and books, and we talked to our accountants, lawyers, customers and suppliers. These helped—but they were not enough! We knew there had to be more, and we were aware that larger companies provided their leaders with the internal and external growth tools that were inaccessible to us.

Initially, we were angry. It didn't seem fair. We worked as hard or harder than these large company managers. We believed we were as smart and as innovative. But we lacked ready access to advice, mentors, and coaching. So, we decided to do something about it.

Larry reached out to the CEOs of some of the world's most successful companies at that time (including Southwest Airlines, Nucor Steel, Home Depot, and Progressive Insurance) and asked if they would be willing to meet with him and share their secrets. Surprisingly, many of them agreed.

Laurence chose a different path. He became a junior partner in Tumi, applied what he observed larger companies doing, and developed a formula that created unprecedented growth in that industry. This led to executive-level positions at large businesses that were divisions of major public companies (including Coach, a division of Sara Lee, and Elizabeth Arden, a division of Unilever).

Jennifer pursued a sales and sales management career at multiple consumer products companies and subsequent consulting clients, including small or closely held businesses and global companies. She learned to navigate countless situations to drive growth through creativity, flexibility and perseverance.

Our life and work "in the trenches" gave us an inside look at the tools and techniques these great companies were using. Over the next 20 years, we applied our own styles and philosophies to what we had learned, creating distinctive approaches to business leadership and growth. The results were significant.

After operating a construction products and services business, Larry founded a consulting practice and eventually became the Management Consulting practice leader at BDO, a global accounting, tax and advisory services company. Laurence, in addition to his executive roles as president of Coach, EVP and general manager at Elizabeth Arden, and CEO of Tumi, was invited to join the boards of several leading consumer brands, usually with private equity or institutional investors. Through Jennifer's work as a salesperson and a sales leader, she refined the SOAR approach to sales growth to create usable tools for accelerated growth.

We standardized our approaches to growth and value creation, documented our unique tools and techniques, and created a system and methodology that has evolved into the SOAR program.

Conclusion

Our journey in the pursuit of business growth has been shaped by passion, perseverance, and a deep desire to make meaningful contributions to the companies we've served. Through decades of hands-on experience, we have honed the principles, tools, and methodologies that form the foundation of the SOAR program. What began as a personal quest to bridge the gap between small and medium-sized businesses and their larger competitors has grown into a comprehensive system for driving growth, creating value, and unlocking potential.

Chapter 4
Introduction to SOAR

Our careers have spanned over 40 years as executives and consultants at companies including Price Waterhouse, BDO, the Parkland Group, Tumi, and Coach. We have helped develop and implement growth plans at hundreds of businesses.

1. There are more than seven hundred strategic initiatives that can build the foundation for business growth. *We have identified and cataloged these, and they have become the key driver of SOAR. To our knowledge, this has never been done before or since.*

2. The possible strategic initiatives can be broadly grouped into what we call the SOAR Four Pillars of Growth, shown on the next page. In essence, it isn't just about growing sales and margins. While the Sales and Margins Pillar generates a majority of the growth potential, significant and valuable growth initiatives or foundations can be achieved by pursuing initiatives in the other pillars.

3. Most businesses only have the bandwidth to pursue between five and ten strategic growth initiatives at the same time.

4. Most businesses need an organized and structured process to identify the best "unmet needs" to pursue. In SOAR parlance, we call these "Opportunities," which are the best ways to grow revenues, margins, and earnings.

5. In addition to pursuing optimal Opportunities, most businesses also need a process to identify and implement "Necessities," which are the actions that facilitate successfully executing the Opportunities and help protect, preserve, and strengthen the organization.

In the chapters that follow, we will explore SOAR's Four Pillars of Growth more fully, giving you the knowledge and tools to unlock your business's full potential.

SOARgrowth is built around the SOAR Four Pillars of Growth:

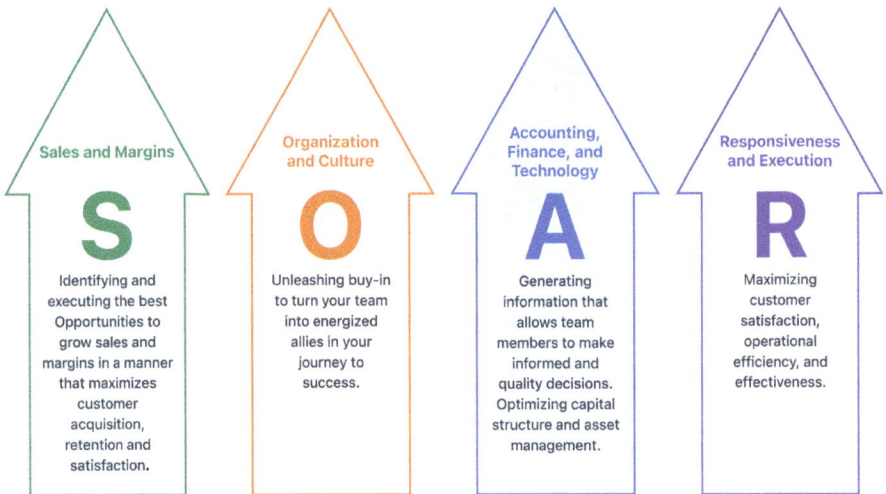

Sales and Margins	Organization and Culture	Accounting, Finance, and Technology	Responsiveness and Execution
S	**O**	**A**	**R**
Identifying and executing the best Opportunities to grow sales and margins in a manner that maximizes customer acquisition, retention and satisfaction.	Unleashing buy-in to turn your team into energized allies in your journey to success.	Generating information that allows team members to make informed and quality decisions. Optimizing capital structure and asset management.	Maximizing customer satisfaction, operational efficiency, and effectiveness.

Conclusion

The SOAR methodology is designed around the Four Pillars of Growth: Sales and Margins, Organization and Culture, Accounting, Finance and Technology, and Responsiveness and Execution.

These pillars form the foundation of a structured, comprehensive approach to driving business growth. By addressing all aspects of a business—not just sales and margins but also the underlying operations, team dynamics, and financial strategies—SOAR provides a balanced and holistic path to growth.

Through the SOAR process, in a few hours, businesses can identify the most impactful Opportunities to pursue and the essential Necessities to implement, ensuring that each initiative is both strategically aligned and practically achievable. By focusing on these four pillars, you can uncover hidden potential, streamline your efforts, and pursue sustainable growth. The SOAR framework simplifies complexity, helping you transform over seven hundred potential strategies into a focused plan of action tailored to your unique business needs.

Chapter 5

Painting Your Business's Growth Picture

Leaders set the tone for growth by crafting a clear and inspiring vision for the future.

The starting point is "painting a picture" of what is possible—helping managers and employees get a vivid glimpse into the future so they can visualize what the company might look like at the end of the "planning period" (we suggest three to five years) and have a taste of what the future could yield. This is often what is referred to as the company's "vision."

The picture of the future should be both compelling and achievable, balancing ambition with realism. It might include new products, services, market segments, regions, distribution channels, acquisitions, skills, culture, values, systems, controls, new capabilities, and many other activities. But each of these Opportunities—individually and especially cumulatively—should create value for the business. Naturally, some of these outcomes will be easier to attain than others. But even those requiring significant stretches should be discussed, as these often add significant value.

Turning Vision into Shared Commitment

Some managers and employees will likely be very excited and motivated about the picture leaders are painting. Others might feel overwhelmed, confused, concerned, or skeptical. They may see the picture as being too ambitious or unrealistic. Good leaders will encourage the team to "suspend disbelief" and focus more on whether the picture is attractive and desirable and less on whether it seems achievable right now.

We have found it can be a mistake to short-change your vision based on current assumptions, capabilities, and conditions. With enough passion, creativity, and diligence, skills and resources can often be upgraded to make an attractive and desirable vision become a reality. And yes, there are times when the team will conclude that the picture is too bold, and only a select few of those Opportunities should be tackled—and can be achieved with the company's current capabilities. But if you don't begin by aiming high, great Opportunities may elude you because the team was not challenged to push beyond their comfort zone.

When leaders are presenting the picture to the team, it is vitally important to give the team time to absorb the ideas and concepts. The team must be encouraged to ask questions, express reservations, and make suggestions. A good technique is to ask the quietest person in the room what they are thinking or their response to what they have heard. A collaborative approach invariably produces a better vision—and helps generate buy-in, which is a powerful contributor to business success.

Addressing Necessities: Building the Foundation for Growth

In addition to the picture involving the pursuit of the most attractive Opportunities, the team will likely conclude that there are also Necessities that must be tackled to enable Opportunities to become realities. These may include new systems, controls, skills, facilities, equipment, team additions, and organizational behaviors.

From Vision to Action

Once the leaders and the team achieve consensus on the future picture, the team must work backward and determine what actions are necessary now and in the future to help the picture become reality. Milestones, action plans, timelines, responsibilities, and budgets must be developed. We have found that it is best to tackle Opportunities and Necessities separately, as they can require different approaches, diligence, and skill sets.

From Abstract Vision to Strategic Clarity

The picture of the company's future usually starts out like an impressionist painting—with many aspects not crystal clear. As the team proceeds with planning and implementation, things invariably become clearer. The vision may be refined, and the Opportunities and Necessities may change in the degree of difficulty, attractiveness, and priority. Evolving internal and external conditions and circumstances can also impact the picture. This requires that the picture and implementation plans be monitored and evaluated continuously—and updated and adapted as circumstances unfold and the picture becomes clearer.

Successfully navigating the path from strategy to execution is what separates high-performing businesses from the rest of the pack. Painting the picture of the future in a collaborative culture is exciting and motivating. The diligent development and execution of implementation plans are usually not as much fun. However, both are essential to growth.

Painting the Picture

Company leaders who want to achieve growth have two strategic paths: "go with the flow," or "planned growth."

Many businesses default to going with the flow. They might work very hard, but they don't have a clear definition of where they are heading, how they are going to get there, and why the strategy is likely to work.

SOAR companies choose planned growth. They do this by:

- Having an honest and realistic assessment of their Current State— good and bad.
- "Painting a clear picture" of their desired Future State. This is one of leadership's most important responsibilities and is a key to successful growth.

Team members (and all stakeholders, including shareholders, suppliers, and lenders) will be in a significantly stronger position to help the business succeed if they have a clear understanding of "where" the business is heading.

"Painting the picture" means conceptualizing the Future State of the business and describing the journey from the Current State to the Future State.

Defining how the business is going to evolve from its Current State to the desired Future State, SOAR uses two key concepts to define the "how":

1. Opportunities, which are the best ways to grow revenues, margins, and earnings. This will likely include clearly defining which products, market segments, and channels the company pursues to facilitate moving from the Current State to the Future State.

   It could also include non-organic growth opportunities, like acquisitions, joint ventures, partnerships, and alliances.

   In addition, improvements in productivity and reductions in cost also represent growth opportunities in that they contribute to growing earnings.

   To qualify as an Opportunity, the initiative must have the potential to have a direct and positive impact on the company's profitability.

2. Necessities, which are actions that facilitate successfully executing the Opportunities and help protect, preserve, and strengthen the organization.

The journey consists of selecting the most relevant Opportunities and Necessities that take the business from what would occur if market forces were left alone to impact the business to what can occur by successfully executing the plan.

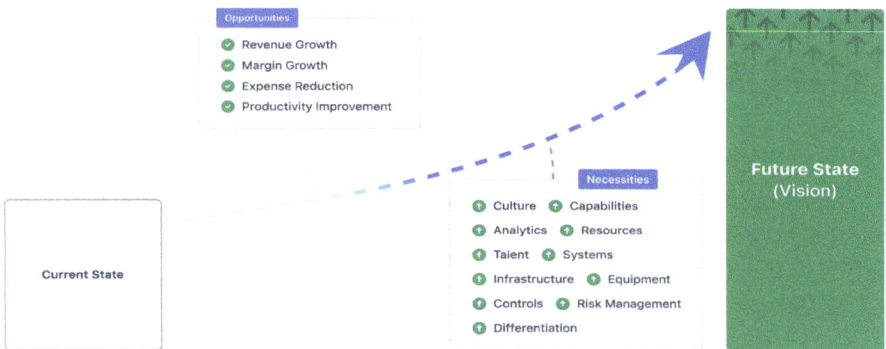

The Future State should represent the business scope and impact three to five years in the future in a compelling manner and with enough specificity to guide decision-making, resource allocation, and risk management.

Leaders set the tone for growth by crafting a clear and inspiring vision for the future. The starting point is "painting a picture" of what is possible—helping managers and employees get a vivid glimpse into the future.

If the Future State is properly drafted and communicated, the team should all be able to visualize it clearly ("where") and understand both "how" and "why" it is likely to work.

Leaders have the responsibility to communicate why implementing the Opportunities and Necessities is the most appropriate action to lead the organization to the Future State and that they are realistic, believable, and doable within the company's bandwidth (financial, technical, and organizational capabilities).

Creating buy-in for managers and team members is a key ingredient to attaining the outcomes the plan articulates.

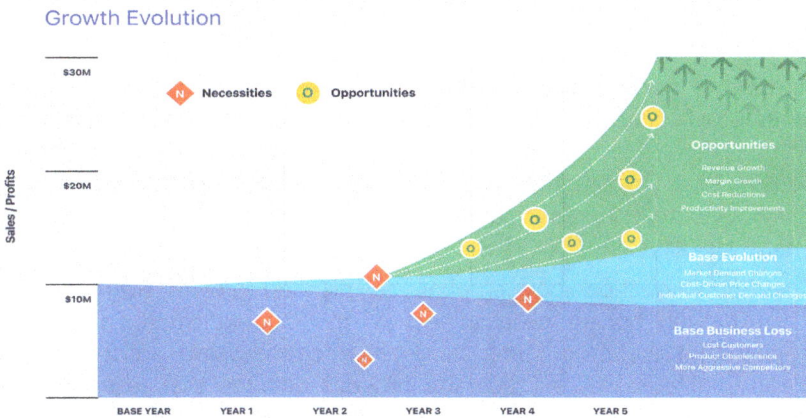

Growth Evolution

The graphic above provides a visual description of how business growth evolution works.

The dark blue section represents the Base Business Loss, which is a snapshot of the business currently—its products, markets, capabilities, strengths, weaknesses, challenges, and threats. The Base Business reflects the company's expectations for how the business will unfold over the next few years without new strategic initiatives. In many cases, the Base Business will decline due to customers leaving or scaling back, product obsolescence, and aggressive or more effective competitors.

The light blue section represents the Base Evolution, reflecting the impact of changes in market demand, individual customer demand changes, and cost-driven price changes. These changes can be positive or negative.

The combination of your Base Business Loss and Base Evolution creates a view of the revenues and earnings of your business over the next few years—*if you do not implement any new strategic initiatives.*

The darker green section reflects what could happen to your business when you identify and implement new Opportunities that drive sales and margin growth and/or reduce costs, thereby improving overall sales and earnings.

The red diamond shapes with an N represent the implementation of Necessities that will enable business success and revenue growth. Without these, the success of planned Opportunities could be hindered, and the business could become vulnerable to risks, threats, and weaknesses.

The combination of your Base Business Loss, Base Evolution, Opportunities, and Necessities paints a picture of what your business could become with a dedicated and committed effort to understand and manage all of these key growth elements according to the SOAR growth pillars.

Conclusion

Painting a clear and compelling picture of your business's future is a cornerstone of successful growth. It provides a shared vision that inspires and aligns the entire organization, giving purpose and direction to daily activities. By defining both Opportunities and Necessities, leaders create a roadmap that not only drives revenue and margin growth but also builds the foundation for long-term sustainability.

The SOAR methodology emphasizes planned growth over accidental growth. Through honest assessments of the Current State and strategic definitions of the Future State, businesses can develop actionable plans that are ambitious yet realistic. The process ensures that team members understand the "where," "how," and "why" of the journey, creating buy-in and fostering a collaborative culture.

Growth is an evolution, and with the right mix of vision, planning, and execution, businesses can transform challenges into achievements and aspirations into tangible results. By following the SOAR principles, you can turn your growth picture into a reality, positioning your business for enduring success.

Chapter 6
The SOAR Growth Engine™

SOAR's approach to sales growth is driven by the SOAR Growth Engine™, a proprietary process we have developed and refined through years of hands-on experience and research.

The Growth Engine maps the potential growth journey of a business from its current base (typically the previous year's or past 12 months' performance) to the desired outcomes at the end of the planning period, which is usually 3-5 years, but can extend up to a decade.

Base Business Loss

Every business faces "base business losses", which arise from lost customers, reduced purchasing from existing customers, product obsolescence, declining value propositions, and competition from more aggressive or effective rivals.

To achieve meaningful growth, businesses must plan for this inevitable churn. By anticipating potential losses and factoring them into strategic initiatives, companies can ensure they generate enough new growth to not only offset churn but also meet their overall growth objectives.

SOAR Growth Engine™

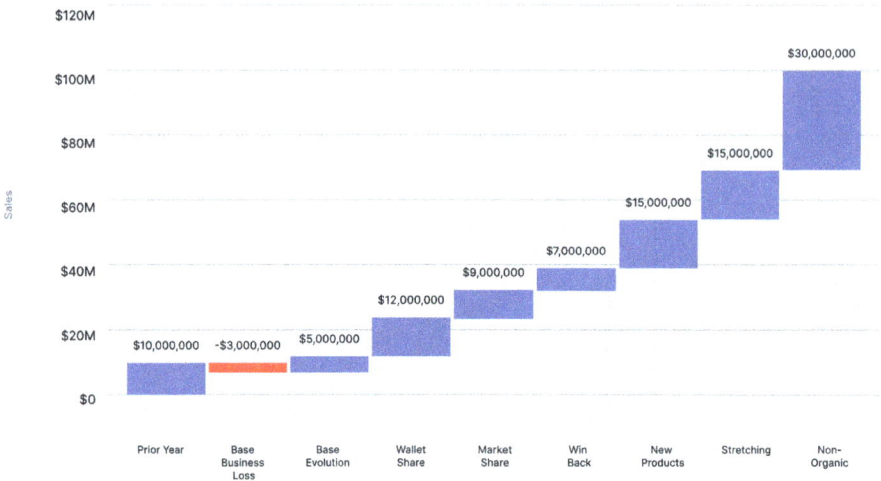

Base Evolution

Base evolution refers to the natural trajectory a business can expect without implementing any new strategic initiatives. In this scenario, the company's growth—or decline—is shaped predominantly by external factors rather than deliberate, strategic actions.

The following external events can impact base business evolution:

A. Market demand

Riding the wave of market demand is what is likely to happen to a business without any new strategic initiatives. The business rises or falls with the momentum of the wave. If the momentum is positive, the business is likely to grow. If the momentum is negative, the business could shrink.

Riding the wave is an effective way to grow sales when external conditions are favorable. However, this strategy requires more than just luck. Companies must actively position themselves to capitalize on the positive trends and (as the example below demonstrates) establish the basis for continued growth if the market reverses itself.

Example: Peloton

Peloton's business model offered "connected fitness" equipment paired with live-streamed classes for at-home use. They capitalized on the wave of demand for home fitness during the COVID-19 pandemic. With gyms closed and people seeking to stay active at home, Peloton saw an explosion in both sales of equipment and the related subscription for its services. As a result, the company became a household name. Peloton invested heavily in their digital platform and creating a strong community around their brand, trusting that this would ensure that they could both ride the wave and build lasting customer loyalty.

However, when COVID-19 declined, connected fitness receded in the minds of many people who enjoyed working out as a social activity in addition to a physical one. Operating issues (being over-inventoried and having new product failures) plus the reduction in their subscriber base left Peloton with serious liquidity issues. The founder-led culture was slow to adapt, and finally, the board brought in new management to try to salvage and grow the business.

B. Price increases

In an inflationary environment, most businesses will be able to grow by simply raising prices. In some cases, this may be due to cost increases that the business is passing on to its customers. In other cases, the business may be able to implement price increases due to increasing market demand. This happened extensively during the COVID-19 pandemic. Many businesses were able to experience price growth in excess of their cost increases due to supply chain shortages.

C. High-growth customers

Some businesses are able to grow significantly because their customers are growing faster than their competitors.

NVIDIA and Intel, two leading semiconductor companies, have exhibited contrasting growth trajectories in recent years. NVIDIA has been achieving significant growth rates, while Intel's sales have been declining. A significant portion of NVIDIA's growth is attributed to its data center segment, driven by demand for AI and data analytics solutions, a market segment that is not a strength for Intel. As a result, suppliers to NVIDIA are likely to experience higher sales growth than Intel suppliers.

Six Major Growth Paths

From our extensive analysis, we have determined that there are six major ways a business can grow sales revenue - in addition to being able to "ride the wave of growth" if they enjoy a positive Base Evolution. They are depicted in the Growth Engine chart above, which shows the path used by a business to grow from a base of $10 million to $100 million.

Most of the six growth drivers are supported by multiple sub-components, increasing the range of Opportunities for creating growth. The SOAR process helps each business pinpoint its most relevant and impactful growth Opportunities while also identifying the most critical Necessities required to successfully execute its plan.

There are six major ways a business can grow sales revenue - in addition to being able to "ride the wave of growth" if they enjoy a positive Base Evolution.

Prioritize Easier Growth Opportunities

The SOAR Growth Engine™ is thoughtfully structured to reflect the relative degree of difficulty for each growth initiative, progressing from left to right. Typically, strategies on the left are more straightforward to implement, while those on the right require greater effort, complexity, and risk. For most businesses, it is prudent to prioritize and optimize the simpler growth opportunities first, building a strong foundation before advancing to more challenging initiatives.

The Six Components of the SOAR Growth Engine™

1. Increasing Wallet Share

Increasing wallet share—doing more business with existing customers—is often overlooked in favor of customer acquisition. However, research shows that existing customers are far more valuable than new ones. It is several times more costly and difficult to attract a new customer than to retain an existing one. Increasing wallet share can lead to significant growth with relatively low acquisition costs.

There are **three different ways to increase your wallet share**, each with different execution strategies:

Type of Wallet Share	Description	Strategies
A	Sell more of the products you are **currently selling** to the customer.	<ul><li>Ask the customer what it will take to receive a bigger share of their buying dollars</li><li>Offer volume discounts</li><li>Promote or improve features and benefits</li><li>Enhance terms and conditions</li></ul>
B	Sell products **you currently offer** but that the customer is **not buying from you.**	<ul><li>Offer promotional pricing</li><li>Offer bundled pricing</li><li>Offer a liberal return policy</li><li>Offer to sell on consignment</li></ul>
C	Sell products **you do not currently offer** but could bring to market.	<ul><li>Explore the feasibility and cost of manufacturing the product or delivering the service</li><li>Alternatively, consider outsourcing to another supplier</li></ul>

Example: Starbucks' Loyalty Program

Starbucks' loyalty program, combined with new product development, allowed the company to significantly increase wallet share in all categories (A, B, and C). Customers who use the Starbucks app accumulate points with every purchase. The points can be redeemed for free drinks and other perks. The app not only incentivizes repeat purchases but also provides Starbucks with valuable data about customer preferences, allowing them to offer personalized deals, test new items, and update their menus. By building customer loyalty, encouraging frequent visits, and introducing higher-priced offerings, Starbucks has increased the amount each customer spends.

2. Expanding Market Share

Expanding market share is about winning new customers within your current markets and products or services. The result is that your sales grow at a rate that is stronger than the market trend because you are growing your share of the market. In most cases, it is more difficult to grow market share than to grow wallet share, as it requires the acquisition of new customers who might not be familiar with your company or who might be loyal to your competitors.

Example: Spotify Gaining Market Share in Music Streaming

Spotify increased its market share by offering a "freemium" model that allowed users to stream music for free with ads, while premium users could pay for an ad-free experience. This helped attract customers who were hesitant to pay for a streaming service upfront with a "try it; you'll like it" approach. Additionally, Spotify used technology and data analysis to focus on personalizing and enhancing the experience with recommendations and curated playlists. As a result, Spotify has become a leader in the music streaming market with consistent user and subscriber gains.

3. Customer Win-Back

Winning back lost customers can be an efficient way to regain revenue and strengthen relationships. It's frequently easier to reconnect with someone who has already done business with you than to convince a new prospect to take a chance on your product.

A subcomponent of win-back is identifying and recapturing customers who have scaled their purchases back.

Both require an understanding of why the customer left or scaled back and the development of tailored programs to address their concerns.

Example: Comcast's Win-Back Campaign

Comcast, a large telecom company, launched a win-back campaign to recover customers who had switched to other internet service providers. By offering special promotions, addressing service issues, and providing incentives like free premium channels, Comcast was able to win back a significant number of lost customers. The company also improved its customer service processes to minimize future churn.

Another subcomponent of Win-Back is rejuvenating older products that have declined in sales or fallen out of favor. With the appropriate product upgrades and promotional strategies, it is often possible to generate growth from older products.

Example: Ford Mustang

The Ford Mustang, first launched in 1964, became a cultural icon in the American car industry. Over the years, interest in the Mustang waned, especially as fuel-efficient and compact cars gained popularity. In 2005, Ford rejuvenated the Mustang brand by introducing a redesigned model that blended retro styling with modern technology, targeting both car enthusiasts and a younger generation of drivers. The introduction of the electric vehicle (EV) version of the Ford Mustang in 2020 has also had a significant positive impact on the Mustang brand, generating sales to a different consumer segment without cannibalizing sales of the traditional Mustang.

4. New Products and Services

Introducing new products or services is a higher-risk, higher-reward growth strategy. It involves research and development, testing, quality control, marketing, and gaining market acceptance. The chances of success are uncertain, but if executed well, new product launches can significantly boost revenue.

Different types of new products include:

- **Incremental:** Improvements or enhancements to existing products, such as toothpaste with whitening or detergent with easy-to-use upgraded packaging.
- **Extensions:** Variations of the same basic product or service, such as Levi's offering new colors, sizes, and styles.
- **Adjacencies:** Related products that complement existing offerings, such as Adidas offering apparel along with its core footwear lines
- **Disruptive:** Game-changing innovations that alter the competitive landscape, such as Netflix superceding its own disruptive DVD by mail model with video streaming technology.
- **New Uses:** Leveraging existing products or technology for new applications, such as aspirin's role in heart health or Tesla's use of battery technology to create a home electricity storage and generator system.
- **New:** A completely new product or service which might not fit with the current range, such as Post-it Notes. Launched in 1980, this was a product that previously did not exist and has been a huge success for 3M.

While disruptive and new innovations can lead to groundbreaking success, incremental and extension-based products are often more manageable and can still deliver substantial growth.

Example: Apple Growing via New Product Development

Apple has repeatedly proven its ability to grow through new product launches. One of the most notable examples is the introduction of the iPhone in 2007, which transformed the mobile phone market. The iPhone quickly became Apple's flagship product, driving the company's growth and increasing its market share in the smartphone industry. Similarly, Apple's foray into wearables with the Apple Watch and AirPods has contributed billions in revenue, further showcasing its ability to innovate and grow through new product development.

5. Stretching

Stretching involves stepping out of a business's comfort zone by exploring new segments, geographies, or channels. This strategy carries a high degree of difficulty but can offer significant rewards when successfully implemented.

- **Segments:** Expanding from one industry to another, such as moving from automotive to aerospace.
- **Geography:** Entering new regions, whether a new suburb, city, or state—or even a different country.
- **Channels:** Diversifying sales channels by adding e-commerce, direct sales, franchising, or other distribution channels to the mix.

Example: SpaceX and Starlink

While leading Tesla to revolutionize the electric vehicle industry, Elon Musk stretched his business horizons by advancing SpaceX and launching Starlink. SpaceX, founded by Musk in 2002, focuses on reducing space transportation costs and enabling the colonization of Mars. In 2015, under SpaceX, he initiated Starlink—a project to deploy a constellation of satellites providing global high-speed internet coverage. Through these ventures, Musk stretched his business focus from sustainable energy to aerospace and global communications.

Example: Walmart's E-Commerce Development

Walmart expanded its distribution channels by significantly investing in e-commerce to compete with Amazon. In 2016, Walmart acquired Jet.com for $3.3 billion to strengthen its online presence and tap into a younger, tech-savvy customer base. The company enhanced its website and mobile app, offering a wider selection of products and improving user experience. Walmart also launched Walmart+, a subscription service providing benefits such as free shipping and fuel discounts, similar to Amazon Prime. By integrating its vast network of physical stores with its online platform—through services like curbside pickup and same-day delivery—Walmart created a seamless omnichannel experience, effectively bridging the gap between traditional retail and e-commerce.

Example: Tumi's Shift to Omnichannel Sales

Tumi traditionally relied on wholesale arrangements with specialty and department stores. However, as the Tumi brand grew stronger and the company broadened its assortment to generate higher lifetime consumer purchases, much of Tumi's distribution could not offer the brand presence the company desired or the market warranted. As a result, Tumi focused on partnerships where they could install shop-in-shops, and as these proved successful, it added its own retail stores and then e-commerce to complement wholesale points of sale. At the same time, Tumi backed its brand with customer service policies and consistent pricing, providing consumers with a risk-free choice of buying where they preferred to shop. The combination of having a retail presence and an e-commerce site—where consumers could experience the most dynamic aspects of the brand and also still be featured at key third-party retailers—accelerated revenues such that Tumi emerged as both a sales and brand leader in the US and internationally.

6. Non-Organic Growth

The final category focuses on non-organic growth, which involves expansion through external means, such as strategic hires, joint ventures, alliances, licensing, franchises, or acquisitions. Non-organic growth can provide a rapid boost in revenue, but it generally carries a higher degree of difficulty and risk than internally generated growth.

Example: Facebook (Meta) Acquiring Instagram

In 2012, Facebook acquired Instagram for $1 billion, marking one of the most successful non-organic growth strategies in tech history. At the time of the acquisition, Instagram had only 30 million users, but Facebook recognized its potential. The acquisition allowed Facebook to diversify its social media offerings and enter the rapidly growing photo-sharing market. Today, Instagram has over two billion users, and its advertising revenue contributes significantly to Meta's overall business.

Example: Disney and Merchandise Licensing

Disney has used licensing agreements to expand the reach of its characters and franchises into merchandise, from toys and clothing to home goods and games. By licensing well-known characters like Mickey Mouse and products tied to films like Frozen, Disney earns royalties without having to manufacture or distribute these products.

Example: Starbucks and Barnes & Noble

Starbucks and Barnes & Noble formed an alliance with Starbucks coffee shops inside Barnes & Noble bookstores. This partnership helped both companies attract customers to their spaces and created a more inviting environment for book shoppers.

Example: Subway

Subway's franchising model contributed to its rapid expansion, making it one of the largest fast-food chains in terms of locations. Subway kept initial franchise fees and startup costs relatively low, attracting a large number of franchisees. By leveraging this approach, Subway entered small markets that other fast-food giants had overlooked, resulting in over 35,000 stores worldwide.

The SOAR Growth Engine™ provides a structured, multi-faceted approach to driving business growth. Whether it is riding a favorable market wave, increasing share, winning back customers, launching new products, stretching into new markets, or pursuing non-organic growth, businesses have many avenues to explore. However, it is essential to pick the right strategies tailored to the company's specific needs and strengths.

By positioning the sales team for success and selecting the appropriate growth strategies, businesses can achieve sustainable and profitable growth, ensuring long-term success in an ever-changing market.

Conclusion

The SOAR Growth Engine™ offers a comprehensive framework for exploring business growth by leveraging six distinct drivers. Each component—from maximizing the potential of your base business to exploring new products, markets, and non-organic opportunities—serves as a potential pathway to expanding revenues, improving margins, and securing long-term success.

This methodology emphasizes the importance of tailoring growth strategies to your company's unique needs, strengths, and market conditions. By focusing on both organic and non-organic growth opportunities and balancing innovation with operational excellence, businesses create the potential to overcome challenges, adapt to market changes, and unlock untapped opportunities.

The SOAR Growth Engine™ is not just a guide—it's a powerful tool that empowers businesses to prioritize their efforts, execute with precision, and explore growth in a structured, deliberate manner.

Chapter 7

Turning Hypotheses into Reality

Most Opportunities start as **hypotheses**, which the Oxford Dictionary defines as "a supposition made on the basis of limited evidence as a starting point for further investigation."

Essentially, at their inception, Opportunities are educated suggestions. The key team members who participate in the SOAR pursuit of growth determine that a specific action (for example, the development of a new product) could result in improved sales revenue and earnings.

As they and their colleagues explore this potential Opportunity further, they may develop quantitative and qualitative estimates of what the new Opportunity could yield to the business. For example, the new product line could add $5 million in sales and $1 million in earnings within three to five years.

Example: Zappos

Zappos' founder, Nick Swinmurn, developed a hypothesis that people are willing to buy shoes online, even without trying them on, if they have a strong return policy. He initially tested the hypothesis by posting pictures of shoes from local shoe stores online. When someone made a purchase, he bought the shoes from the store and shipped them to the customer. This allowed him to validate demand without investing heavily in inventory upfront.

To take the Opportunity from a hypothesis to reality, the team will likely go through the following key steps:

1. Validation

Intelligence—gaining knowledge to make an informed decision. This includes estimating the size and potential growth rate of the market for the Opportunity.

- Understanding the current competitors and their market positions, strengths, and weaknesses.
- Estimating the cost, time, and degree of difficulty to develop the Opportunity.
- Interviewing customers and prospects to gauge their reaction to the Opportunity.

If possible, conduct a Beta Test of the Opportunity or receive feedback based on samples or prototypes.

- Have customers and prospects take the Opportunity on a "test drive" and provide tangible feedback regarding the attractiveness and feasibility of the Opportunity.
- A key piece of information to be gathered is whether customers or prospects perceive the Opportunity as attractive—offering features and benefits that current sources do not offer—and attribute a value that will allow the business to earn an acceptable margin and return on its investment.

Using this information, leadership can make a preliminary decision whether the Opportunity is a worthwhile investment for the company.

2. Development of an action plan, which includes:

- Determining and documenting the detailed steps needed to implement the Opportunity. This is frequently done by a team of people who are led by an Opportunity champion (or team leader), who has the ultimate responsibility and accountability for the development and implementation of the Opportunity. Ideally, the team is made up of a cross-functional group of three to ten members representing the key functions involved who are capable, collaborative, and committed to effectively bringing the Opportunity to life on time and on budget.

- Developing the timetable and budget.
- Developing the proposed value proposition, costing, pricing, sales and marketing plans, and related operations and infrastructure requirements.

3. **Implementation of the action plan.**

As the implementation of the action plan begins and continues, validation moves to a different level. This is the first time the Opportunity is truly tested in the real world,

- In this phase, the Opportunity is validated by customers and prospects issuing purchase orders and writing real checks.

4. **Modification of the action plan based on evolving information, obstacles, and pivots.**

- The Validation and Implementation phases invariably reveal shortcomings, challenges, obstacles, and surprises—hopefully, some good and perhaps some not-so-good.
- Often customers and prospects see pros and cons in the Opportunity that were not evident to the company.
- Frequently, the company learns that it misjudged the market demand and pricing. It could be higher or lower than originally anticipated.
- The company might also learn more about competing products that may impact the likely success of the Opportunity.
- All this information usually requires the company to make some changes or pivots to the Opportunity design or the pricing, marketing, or sales plan.
- This information can also cause the company to rethink the priority of the Opportunity. They may have previously considered this Opportunity to be the third-best Opportunity, but they may now move it to the number one or two position.
- Occasionally, the feedback is bad enough for the company to decide to move the opportunity way down on the priority list—or even remove it from the list completely.

Developing and harvesting Opportunities is not a static process. The selected Opportunities and Necessities need to be regularly and consistently evaluated and updated. Opportunities may yield more or less than expected. They can be accelerated, modified, or curtailed. External and internal factors may require a shift in priorities.

Dynamic process

Unfortunately, many businesses start implementation without validation or development of a realistic action plan. SOAR companies learn that taking the time and discipline to do things properly invariably increases the odds of successful growth, as does rigorous follow-up on how the action teams are doing and what modifications to the team and the plan need to be made based on actual results and learnings.

Transforming hypotheses into reality can be a challenging yet exciting and rewarding journey and we've developed a proven step-by-step methodology (visit SOARgrowth.com to learn about a digital version) to make the process clear and achievable for your business. It requires dedication and effort, but a proven and collaborative team-based process can streamline the journey and make the workload far more manageable.

SOAR companies feature "continuous strategic thinking," where key leaders, managers, and team members are trained and encouraged to regularly debate and propose possible new Opportunities and Necessities as well as evaluate the effectiveness of current ones.

When the discussion, debate, and implementation of Opportunities and Necessities become part of daily life in a business, the company will be powerfully positioned to capitalize on its growth potential.

Developing and harvesting Opportunities is not a static process.
The selected Opportunities and Necessities need to be regularly
and consistently evaluated and updated.

Conclusion

Turning a hypothesis into reality is the essence of growth and innovation. The journey from identifying a potential Opportunity to successfully implementing it requires validation, careful planning, disciplined execution, and continuous adaptation. It's a dynamic process that thrives on strategic thinking, cross-functional collaboration, and a willingness to learn from successes and setbacks.

By following a structured approach—validating assumptions, creating robust action plans, and refining strategies based on real-world feedback—businesses can significantly enhance their odds of success. This approach ensures that Opportunities are not only pursued but are also positioned to deliver measurable value. With the right mindset, tools, and dedication, your company can transform educated guesses into actionable strategies that drive long-term growth and success.

By embedding the pursuit of Opportunities and Necessities into the fabric of your organization, you create a culture of innovation, adaptability, and sustained progress, ensuring that your business is always ready to capitalize on its full potential.

Chapter 8
Sales Execution

Sales growth is a cornerstone of business success, yet many organizations struggle to achieve the desired results. The challenge often lies not in the ambition of the goals but in the ability to execute effectively. Sales execution is the bridge between strategy and results—it's where plans transform into action and outcomes.

While businesses often look at surface-level factors like sales calls and closing rates, the answer lies in the holistic alignment of strategy, execution, and company-wide support. Effective sales execution requires more than just a skilled sales team. It demands a comprehensive approach that aligns strategy, training, leadership, tools, and organizational support. Businesses must empower their sales teams with the resources they need, foster collaboration across departments, and ensure a customer-centric approach that delivers exceptional experiences. When executed well, this holistic framework not only drives sales but also strengthens customer loyalty, enhances the company's reputation, and creates a foundation for sustained growth.

1. Sales Training: Beyond Just Selling Skills

When sales performance falters, the immediate reaction is often to question the effectiveness of the sales team: are they making enough calls and closing enough deals? While these are valid concerns, they miss the bigger picture. A more important question is: are we putting our sales team in a position to succeed?

Effective sales training goes far beyond teaching selling techniques. It requires equipping the sales team with comprehensive knowledge about the company's products, market conditions, and customer needs. A well-trained sales team is only as strong as the intelligence, strategy, and tools they are provided.

Many businesses mistakenly treat sales training as a one-time action focused solely on selling techniques. In reality, this should be the final step, not the only step, and training should occur regularly to both energize the team and provide the most current strategies and techniques to succeed.

2. Developing a Winning Sales Strategy

A successful sales strategy focuses on working smarter, not harder. Businesses often overburden their sales teams without optimizing processes, leading to burnout and inefficiency. To avoid this, a clear, well-defined strategy must be established that aligns the entire company with the sales team's goals.

Key elements of a winning sales strategy include:

- **Customer Satisfaction:** Make exceptional service and product quality a core value.
- **Targeted Markets:** Focus on products and markets that are easier to succeed in, such as those with growing demand or higher margins.
- **Ideal Customers:** Clearly define who your ideal customers are and tailor your sales plan around their needs.
- **Differentiation:** Create a compelling value proposition that sets your business apart from competitors (see Chapter 10).
- **Brand Development:** Build strong brand recognition to make prospects more receptive to your sales efforts. Even if you sell unbranded or multiple branded products or services, your company name and reputation are the equivalent of the brand that can differentiate you from your competitors.

Examples:

Amazon is a great example of turning a "marketplace" into a "brand." Although the vast majority of its products are made by others, it is a go-to shopping site for everything from books to entertainment to household appliances and groceries.

Companies such as Salesforce have succeeded by clearly defining their target market and offering a differentiated value proposition that focuses on solving specific customer problems.

3. Keys to Effective Sales Execution

Even the best sales strategy will fail without proper execution. Successful sales execution requires alignment across the organization and providing the tools and support that allow the sales team to succeed. Here are eight critical elements to ensure effective execution:

a. Strong Sales Leadership

- Recruit and hire appropriately qualified salespeople in sufficient numbers, blending hunters (who excel at new business development) and farmers (who manage existing customer relationships).
- Serve as a coach, cheerleader, and motivator for the sales team.
- Remove roadblocks and obstacles to the sales team's success.
- Retain high performers and address consistent underperformers by reassigning or replacing them as needed.

b. Clear Goals and Strategy

- Set clear and attainable sales goals that challenge the team without causing burnout or disengagement.
- Provide the sales team with a clear understanding of the sales strategy and plan.
- Ensure that the team fully understands their roles and responsibilities and the overall sales plan.

c. Motivating Compensation and Incentives

- Develop and implement competitive and motivating compensation structures.
- Reward the sales team with incentives that drive performance toward the company's goals and foster loyalty.

d. Training and Development

- Ensure that the sales team receives appropriate training in the company's products, services, value proposition, and selling skills.
- Offer holistic training so that everyone in the organization understands their role in supporting sales efforts.

e. Tools, Data, and Information Systems

- Equip the sales team with necessary tools and technology, including laptops, customer relationship management (CRM) systems, and market intelligence tools.

- Provide access to relevant data, information systems, and clear lines of communication.
- Use CRM systems to assign qualified leads and track sales activities, goals, and progress.

f. **Effective Marketing Collateral and Website**
- Maintain an effective and comprehensive website that serves as the entry point to the customer acquisition funnel.
- Ensure marketing materials support lead generation and customer acquisition efforts.
- Use engaging content, calls-to-action, and lead-capture forms to attract and convert potential customers.

g. **Lead Generation Systems**
- Implement lead generation strategies such as SEO, social media engagement, advertising (traditional and digital), trade shows, email, SMS, direct mail, and telemarketing.
- Use CRM systems and other digital tools to generate and manage leads and help the sales team work efficiently.

h. **Qualifying Leads**
- Establish processes to qualify leads and determine their fit for the company.
- Assign qualified leads to salespeople, typically hunters, for follow-up and conversion.

i. **Focus on Core Roles**
- Allow salespeople, especially hunters, to concentrate on their primary roles without unnecessary administrative burdens.
- Streamline tasks to maximize time spent on activities that directly contribute to sales growth.

j. **Holistic Organizational Support**
- Foster a company-wide understanding of how each department contributes to sales success.
- Encourage collaboration between sales, customer service, logistics, operations and other teams to support customer acquisition, satisfaction, and retention.

4. **Customer-Centric Approach**

One of the key foundations of sales success is customer satisfaction. This should not just be the responsibility of the sales team but of the entire company. A dedicated customer-centric approach leads to higher retention, cross-selling opportunities, and better word-of-mouth referrals. A business that consistently delivers exceptional customer experiences will not only meet sales targets but also help grow the company's reputation.

Additionally, analyzing **customer churn**—the rate at which customers stop doing business with you—can reveal valuable insights. If churn is high, it indicates that something is wrong, whether it's product quality, customer service, or market fit.

The company should also track and monitor satisfaction with its products and services. Promptly addressing issues will minimize the fallout from quality or service problems. Even the perception of a product fault can damage the business. Take these issues seriously and regularly meet with both the sales team and customers to discuss "how you are doing."

5. Lead Generation and Conversion Optimization

Lead generation is often a bottleneck in the sales process. A lack of qualified leads can cripple a sales team's ability to meet its targets. Businesses must invest in effective lead generation systems, using a combination of SEO, digital advertising, email campaigns, social media, direct mail, telemarketing and trade shows to drive traffic and interest. Sometimes, the company needs to seek out and hire sales staff from the competition or the industry (assuming no legal restrictions such as non-competes or NDAs), as these people bring both contacts and knowledge of where the best opportunities for growth may lie.

However, lead generation is only half of the equation. Companies must also focus on optimizing conversion rates by improving the sales team's closing ratios. This can be achieved through better sales training, enhancing the value proposition, CRM system integration, and tracking performance metrics.

Example:

Mailchimp, an email marketing company, generates leads through high-value content marketing and a freemium model that allows potential customers to test the service before upgrading. This approach, combined with targeted advertising, helps them attract and convert new customers at a high rate.

While businesses often look at surface-level factors like sales calls and closing rates, the answer lies in the holistic alignment of strategy, execution, and company-wide support.

Conclusion

Sales execution is the operational implementation of the sales strategy and growth plan. Achieving successful sales growth and execution requires a multifaceted approach that involves strategy, training, leadership, and customer focus.

Companies that want to see sustained growth must take a 360-degree view of sales performance, addressing not only selling skills but also the tools, processes, and organizational support that drive execution. By focusing on the right customers, equipping sales teams with the tools they need, and ensuring alignment across the organization, businesses can significantly enhance sales effectiveness and drive long-term growth.

Achieving successful sales execution is about more than closing deals—it's about building a system that aligns every aspect of the organization toward growth. From developing a clear strategy and empowering sales teams with the right tools and training to fostering a customer-first mindset across all departments, effective sales execution is the operational heartbeat of the growth engine of a business.

Chapter 9

Good Days Lead to Sales Success and Growth

Closing a large sale is often seen as a clear indicator of success in sales. It gives a salesperson that satisfying feeling of having had a "good day." However, relying on big orders alone is like sprinting at the start of a marathon—it's not sustainable. The key to long-term success is pacing the team, focusing on steady, consistent effort, and accumulating multiple wins over days, weeks, and months.

True sales success comes from consistently creating "good days." Each productive day contributes to a good week, which builds into a strong month, eventually leading to a successful year.

So, how does the company ensure it is having a "good day" every day?

Defining a Good Day

A "good day" in sales can be defined as completing the specific tasks and activities that move the business closer to achieving its sales goals. Often, writing an order is the result of multiple actions, such as:

1. Identifying potential leads.
2. Researching prospects to ensure they're a good fit.

3. Reaching out via phone, email, social media, or direct mail.

4. Attending networking events or trade shows.

5. Engaging in initial conversations with leads.

6. Being invited to present your offering.

7. Holding meetings with prospects.

8. Meeting others in the prospect's organization.

9. Receiving a request for a proposal or quote (RFQ).

10. Helping customers resolve a concern or expedite a shipment.

These activities are just examples of the steps that often occur before an order is finalized. If a salesperson has achieved a targeted number of these activities by the end of the day, they can confidently say, "I had a good day," even if no sales were closed that day.

Tailoring "Good Day" Activities to Your Industry

A "good day" will look different depending on the industry. For example, the daily tasks that drive success in retail are very different from those in manufacturing, construction, or even fitness. It's critical for business leaders to define what a "good day" consists of in their particular field, setting the right activities for their teams to focus on.

Timing Matters

The definition of a "good day" can also vary depending on the time of the week, month, or year. For instance, many businesses prioritize shipping orders toward the end of the month but focus on taking orders earlier in the month. Similarly, industries with seasonal demand, such as horticulture or garden furniture, will have different priorities depending on the time of year.

Sales leadership must remain flexible, ensuring that what constitutes a "good day" aligns with shifting priorities based on timing and demand cycles.

How to Encourage "Good Days"

1. **Set Clear Parameters:** Define what a successful day looks like for your team, keeping in mind the goals and timelines of your business.

2. **Track Progress:** Use tools like a CRM to help salespeople track their daily activities. Clear, visual tracking helps everyone see at a glance whether they've hit their targets.

3. **Create Friendly Competition:** Foster an environment of fun and competition to keep salespeople motivated, with challenges such as who can have the longest streak of consecutive "good days."

The Big Picture: Good Days Lead to Sales Success and Growth

Consistent sales success does not come from sporadic big wins but from executing the right strategy effectively time after time. A strong focus on the key activities that contribute to "good days" will ensure your team is always moving closer to its goals, ultimately driving long-term growth and marketplace gains.

The key to long-term success is pacing the team, focusing on steady, consistent effort, and accumulating multiple wins over days, weeks, and months.

Conclusion

Sales success is built on consistency, not sporadic victories. While closing a large deal is undeniably rewarding, sustainable growth comes from focusing on the daily actions and activities that drive progress toward long-term goals. Defining and fostering "good days"—tailored to your industry, priorities, and timing—ensures that every day contributes to a stronger pipeline and cumulative success.

By setting clear parameters, tracking progress, and fostering motivation through accountability and friendly competition, businesses can cultivate a culture of consistent performance. This disciplined approach transforms "good days" into strong weeks, months, and, ultimately, a successful year.

Sales is a marathon, not a sprint. The key is pacing the team with clear, manageable activities that build momentum over time. When every team member understands and embraces the importance of "good days," the company is better positioned to achieve sustainable growth, strengthen market presence, and secure lasting success.

Chapter 10
Value Proposition and Elevator Pitch

For companies to grow in today's fast-paced business world, the ability to communicate their core values and uniqueness quickly and effectively is paramount for growth. Being a "me-too" company—without any material differentiation—makes significant growth elusive.

Two key tools used for this purpose are the value proposition and the elevator pitch. While often used interchangeably, these are two distinct concepts in communicating a business's reason for being. Understanding the differences between them and knowing how to craft and adapt them are crucial for driving growth in competitive markets.

Understanding the Value Proposition

Your company's **value proposition** should clearly and concisely explain how your products and services provide compelling and differentiated value to the customer. A value proposition is not just about highlighting features but focusing on the value delivered—whether that is improving efficiency, reducing costs, or enhancing customer satisfaction.

Importance of a Strong Value Proposition

A compelling value proposition is essential because it helps a business stand out from its competitors. It provides a solid foundation for all product development, marketing, and sales efforts. Businesses with weak or indistinct value propositions often find their position in the marketplace at a disadvantage, and they are forced to rely on basic selling skills, margin-reducing pricing and discounting, or unprofitable service terms rather than the inherent strengths of the product or service itself.

A strong value proposition ensures that prospects can clearly see how the offering solves their problems and meets their needs better than alternatives. The Value Proposition is the "lens" through which the business views its position in the market and defines its products and services.

Types of Value Propositions

Value propositions can be classified into two main categories:

1. **Product-Based Value Proposition:** This is when the product itself is superior in terms of quality, longevity, ease of use, or other intrinsic features. For example, Apple's iPhones are known for their high-quality build and intuitive software, making them a standout in the smartphone market.

   Example: Uber's Value Proposition

   Uber's value proposition revolves around convenience, reliability, and cost savings. It offers an alternative to traditional taxis by providing a faster, easier, and often cheaper way to get a ride. Uber also benefits from a non-product value proposition, offering users transparency (via the app) on driver location, trip time, and pricing. By combining these factors, Uber created a compelling value proposition that differentiated it from the traditional taxi industry, contributing to its rapid global growth.

2. **Non-Product-Based Value Proposition:** Here, the value is derived from aspects unrelated to the product itself, such as lower prices, better customer service, or more convenient terms.

   Example: Nordstrom

   Nordstrom offered many of the same brands found at its competitors, but through exceptional customer service, a generous return policy, and making the buying process as convenient as possible for customers, it was able to grow from one location in the Pacific Northwest into a national chain.

   Example: Dollar Shave Club

   Dollar Shave Club entered a crowded market with a strong value proposition focused on affordability and convenience: "For a few dollars a month, we deliver great razors right to your door." Its viral elevator pitch, delivered through a humorous video, made the product's unique selling point instantly clear: high-quality razors at a fraction of the cost of traditional brands, without the hassle of shopping. This helped Dollar Shave Club grow rapidly, ultimately leading to its acquisition by Unilever for $1 billion.

The Elevator Pitch: Grabbing Attention Fast

An **elevator pitch** is a short, persuasive statement designed to spark interest in a product, service, or idea. Named for the concept of delivering a compelling idea in the span of an elevator ride, it typically lasts 30 seconds to a minute. The goal of an elevator pitch is not to close a sale but to grab the listener's attention and initiate a deeper conversation.

Importance of a Compelling Elevator Pitch

In networking events, chance encounters, or any setting where time is limited, a well-crafted elevator pitch can be the difference between securing a meeting and being forgotten. An elevator pitch should answer three key questions:

- What problem do you solve?
- How do you solve it better than others?
- What value do you bring to the customer?

An effective elevator pitch may be tailored to the audience, adapting to different scenarios and emphasizing the most relevant points to the listener. For example, a pitch to a company's CFO for your data analytics software could be different from the pitch to that company's head of marketing that got you in the door in the first place.

Even if you have time with your audience for a more comprehensive review of your products, the elevator pitch makes a great introduction to what comes next.

Example: Airbnb's Elevator Pitch

When Airbnb first launched, its elevator pitch was simple and focused: "Airbnb is an online platform that allows people to rent out their extra space to travelers looking for a cheaper and more authentic travel experience." This pitch communicated both the service offered and the unique benefit—access to affordable travel experiences in people's homes rather than traditional hotels. This clear and concise pitch helped Airbnb grow from a small startup to a global hospitality powerhouse.

Crafting and Adapting These Tools

While both the value proposition and elevator pitch are vital, they should not be static. Businesses must continuously update them as markets and technology change, customer needs shift, and the business evolves. Airbnb now serves not only the budget-conscious traveler but also the premium and luxury consumer with multiple types of residences and host services. Their current value proposition encompasses being the most comprehensive and reliable online global marketplace for short-term lodging, serving both owners and renters. Similarly, an elevator pitch must evolve to reflect new developments in the business or changes in the competitive landscape.

Both the elevator pitch and value proposition help a business stand out from the crowd. Companies often overestimate the value they provide, and customers may not always see the business in the same light. High-performing companies take the time to regularly evaluate and improve their value proposition and elevator pitch based on customer feedback and market conditions. Companies that invest in refining these tools are better positioned to capture customer interest and build lasting relationships.

Example: Slack's Adaptation of Its Value Proposition

Slack initially entered the market as a tool for team communication, but over time, it adapted its value proposition to focus on its ability to increase productivity by streamlining collaboration. Slack's value proposition highlights its simplicity, integrations with other tools, and the reduction of internal email traffic. By continuously refining its messaging and understanding the evolving needs of its users, Slack grew to become a major player in workplace communication.

Understanding What Customers Truly Value

The concept of value is subjective—what one customer sees as essential, another may overlook entirely. Even businesses that appear remarkably similar might prioritize very different attributes. One customer may focus on price, while another customer places higher importance on quality, service, or reliability.

To address this variability, businesses should develop a comprehensive matrix of the potential value attributes they offer. This matrix serves as a guide for identifying the unique needs of each customer. By training the sales team to ask insightful, probing questions, they can uncover what the customer truly values and adapt their value proposition accordingly. This tailored approach not only enhances customer satisfaction but also strengthens relationships and improves the likelihood of closing a sale.

Real-World Impact of Value Propositions and Elevator Pitches

Businesses that understand and effectively use value propositions and elevator pitches stand a much greater chance of success in the marketplace. The value proposition and elevator pitch are two critical elements in a company's growth toolkit. While they serve different purposes—one offering depth and the other sparking immediate attention—both need to communicate compelling, differentiated value. Companies that regularly evaluate, refine, and adapt their positioning to meet evolving customer needs and market conditions will be better positioned to succeed in today's competitive landscape.

Position Your Sales Team for Success

A salesperson equipped with a compelling value proposition is far more likely to succeed than one offering a product or service that is only slightly different—or indistinguishable—from those of competitors. In fact, even an average salesperson with a standout value proposition may outperform a highly skilled salesperson selling an undifferentiated offering.

There are two keys to helping your sales team achieve greater success. First and foremost, ensure that they can effectively communicate the value proposition of your current product offering. As stated above, this requires you to identify what customers really value and then shape your value proposition to reinforce your competitive edge and the benefits the customer receives by doing business with you.

A salesperson equipped with a compelling value proposition is far more likely to succeed than one offering a product or service that is only slightly different—or indistinguishable—from those of competitors.

The second is to evaluate if or when your value proposition is no longer as relevant to customers and then decide on what you need to do to reinforce your points of difference in the marketplace. You may choose to upgrade or modify your current products or services or to develop a new product or service that customers are drawn to because it solves their problems or fulfills their needs in a way that stands out from the competition—eliminating the need for heavy persuasion. This may mean going back to the drawing board to enhance your overall offering with better features, stronger benefits, superior service levels, or more appealing terms and conditions. While this may require investment in research, development, and planning, the payoff could be substantial. A strong product offering with a compelling value proposition can significantly improve your sales closing ratios, making it a smart investment to enable growth and long-term success.

Conclusion

A well-defined value proposition and a compelling elevator pitch are indispensable tools for any business seeking growth. Together, they form the foundation of a company's ability to communicate its unique value and competitive edge effectively. While the value proposition delivers a deeper understanding of how the business addresses customer needs, the elevator pitch provides a quick and engaging way to capture attention and open the door to further conversations.

In today's competitive landscape, businesses that invest in crafting and continuously refining these tools are better equipped to differentiate themselves, resonate with their target audience, and adapt to evolving market demands. By understanding what customers truly value and aligning messaging accordingly, companies can enhance customer engagement, drive sales, and build long-lasting relationships. The value proposition and elevator pitch are not just communication tools—they are growth enablers, empowering businesses to position themselves for success in a crowded marketplace.

Chapter 11
Margin Growth

Increasing profit margins can be a very valuable part of the growth plan of a business. While revenue growth is an important goal for most businesses, translating that into profit growth should be the ultimate objective. Higher gross profit margins invariably contribute to higher net profit margins.

For every dollar of sales generated, the goal is to have more profit dollars available to cover selling, general, and administrative expenses—and to generate a net profit for the owners.

In general, the higher your gross profit margin (selling price minus the cost of goods sold), the lower the company's break-even point will be. Your break-even point is the amount of sales revenue you need to generate for your business to break even (no profit but also no loss).

i. Assume that your selling, general, and administrative costs are $300,000 per month.

ii. If your gross profit margin is 50%, you will need to sell $600,000 per month to break even ($300,000/.5).

iii. But if your gross profit margin is 25%, you will need to sell $1,200,000 per month to break even ($300,000/.25).

This is a powerful analysis that demonstrates the benefits and value of working to improve your gross profit margins.

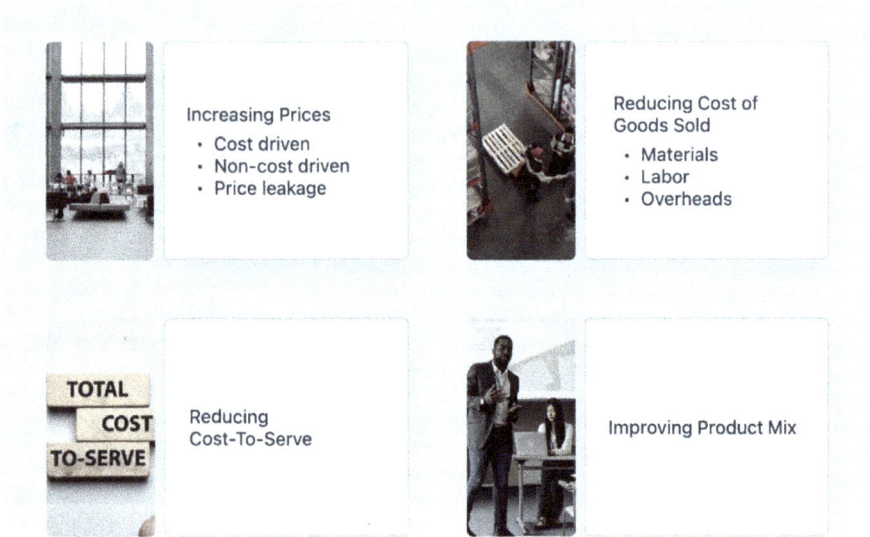

Increasing Prices
- Cost driven
- Non-cost driven
- Price leakage

Reducing Cost of Goods Sold
- Materials
- Labor
- Overheads

Reducing Cost-To-Serve

Improving Product Mix

Gross profit margins can be improved in five different ways: increasing prices, reducing price "leakage," reducing product/service costs, reducing costs-to-serve, and improving product mix.

The goal is, for every dollar of sales generated, to have more profit dollars available to cover selling, general, and administrative expenses— and to generate a net profit for the owners.

---

1. Increasing Prices

There are two reasons why prices could be increased:

- **Cost-driven price increases**

  This involves passing on increases in your product or service costs (materials, labor and overhead costs) to your customers. This is particularly important in inflationary times or when parts of your cost structure experience rapid increases. In many cases, costs are affected by macro events beyond the control of management. For example, in 2021 and 2022 shipping and container rates experienced hyper-increases, and in 2025, the tariff surcharges created unforeseen (and still unanswered challenges for many businesses).

If cost increases are not passed on, the business will likely experience reductions in Gross Profit Margins.

When businesses experience cost increases and they are able to pass on enough of the cost increases to customers in the form of price increases, they generally will merely maintain their Gross Profit Margins rather than increase them. If, however, the business is able to pass on the cost increases and a little more, it could experience a small increase in Gross Profit Margins.

- **Non-cost-driven price increases**

Businesses that are able to increase prices when they are not experiencing cost increases (or are able to pass on cost increases significantly in excess of the price increases) will generally experience significant improvement in gross profit margins.

In general, non-cost-driven price increases can be achieved where:

o Demand for the product or service is strong in relation to the available supply.

o The business is offering significantly more value or better service than most of its competitors.

o Historic prices charged by the company were below those charged by most competitors.

Example: Disney

Disney regularly increases prices for entry to its theme parks and resorts while also raising prices for in-park experiences like food, merchandise, and premium services (e.g., Genie+ service). Additionally, Disney raised prices for its Disney+ streaming service as it expanded its content library with original series and films from Marvel, Star Wars, and other franchises. Disney's gross profit margins in its parks and resorts division improved due to these price increases, and its Disney+ service maintained subscriber growth even after multiple rounds of price hikes. By focusing on exclusive content and customer experience, Disney justified higher prices.

Example: Nike

Nike strategically increased prices on popular products, particularly for premium or limited-edition items such as the Air Jordan line. Nike uses product scarcity and exclusivity to command higher prices, with the perception that these items offer greater value due to their design and limited availability.

2. **Reducing price leakage**

Price leakage occurs when:

- Customers are able to buy at prices that are not justified by the volume of purchases or other factors when compared with other, similar customers.

- Customers are given discounts, promotions, and/or rebates that are not justified by the volume of purchases or other factors when compared with other, similar customers.

- Customers are undercharged for freight, shipping and handling, or other support or services that are not justified by the volume of purchases or other factors when compared with other, similar customers.

Example: Caterpillar

Caterpillar, a leading manufacturer of construction equipment, reduced price leakage by standardizing its pricing across global markets. The company previously faced challenges with inconsistent pricing and unnecessary discounts across different regions, leading to profit erosion. By implementing a global pricing strategy and tightening controls over discounting practices, Caterpillar was able to eliminate price discrepancies and reduce leakage. Caterpillar's gross margins improved as the company captured more value from its equipment sales.

3. **Reducing the Cost of Goods and Services Sold (aka COGS)**

In most businesses, COGS is made up of:

- Materials—the cost of raw materials (like steel, plastic, wire, sugar) or component parts (like motors, semiconductors, circuit boards, wheels).

- Labor—the cost of labor and benefits expended for people involved in producing a product or delivering a service.

- Overheads—the cost of expenses incurred to produce a product or deliver a service (like factory rent, supervisor salaries, equipment maintenance, utility costs).

COGS can be frequently improved by lowering costs in the following areas:

- Materials—improving purchasing and supply chain management; reducing scrap and waste; reducing distances traveled and freight costs; redesigning products to use less or lower-cost materials.

- Labor—improving productivity via continuous improvement or implementing lean techniques, reducing errors, rework, and unnecessary overtime.

- Overheads: reducing occupancy costs by reducing footprint via efficiency or outsourcing; renegotiating insurance costs; reducing supervisory costs via improved training, empowerment, and teamwork; reducing maintenance costs via planned maintenance programs; reducing utility costs via improved energy management.

Example: IKEA

IKEA reduces the cost of materials through bulk purchasing and long-term contracts with suppliers, allowing it to obtain lower prices on raw materials. IKEA also practices vertical integration, owning much of its own supply chain, from forestry operations to manufacturing facilities. This gives the company greater control over material costs and sourcing. IKEA has managed to keep its product prices relatively low while maintaining high gross profit margins by controlling material costs and passing some savings to customers.

4. Reducing Costs-to-Serve

Costs-to-serve are the costs involved in serving a customer that are not captured in COGS. In most businesses, COGS is designed to represent an average cost for all customers. However, in reality, a variety of factors impact the true COGS related to a particular customer, and using averages can create misleading data that can lead to an incorrect determination of COGS and gross profit margins for individual customers.

Some customers are more difficult to serve, and some are easier.

- Some customers are prone to reject or return products even though they meet the company's quality standards, creating significant work for the company to receive, inspect, possibly rework, and replace the products.

- Customers who provide short lead times for their orders—or customers who change or cancel their orders frequently—create more work and challenges than customers who provide long lead times without changes.

- Customers who order in smaller quantities create more work than those who order in larger quantities.

There are more than thirty different types of costs-to-serve. Because most of these are usually not captured in COGS (due to deficiencies in most company's accounting systems), they are often ignored. However, they are very real costs and can have a material impact on the true profit margin earned from a particular customer. As a result, working to understand and reduce costs-to-serve can have a meaningful impact on improving real gross profit margins.

Example: Salesforce

Salesforce, the provider of customer relationship management software, deals with a wide range of customers, from small businesses to large enterprises, many of which require significant support and customization. To manage the costs of serving demanding clients, Salesforce implemented tiered service offerings, where higher-paying customers receive premium support while lower-paying customers are encouraged to use self-service tools. By introducing customer success tools, knowledge bases, and community forums, Salesforce reduced the costs associated with manual customer support. Salesforce's gross profit margins improved as it reduced the costs associated with serving high-maintenance customers.

5. **Improving product mix**

In many businesses, the gross profit margins earned from individual products and product lines vary widely. If a business guides its sales and marketing teams to promote more of the higher gross profit margin items, the company might be able to increase its overall gross profit margins by merely steering its product mix towards more profitable items.

Companies can also ensure that new product or service developments raise the overall margin by building in features that justify higher prices and margins or allow for reduced costs or cost-to-serve, therefore improving mix over time.

Even a small percentage increase in margins can lead to higher overall profitability. For example, if a company has $5 million in revenue, 30% gross profit margins, and a 5% operating margin, it will yield $250,000 in operating earnings. If the gross profit margin improved by just 1%, earnings would increase by $50,000, or 20%.

Conclusion

Increasing gross profit margins is one of the most effective ways to enhance the profitability and overall success of a business. By focusing on the key areas of price increases, reducing price leakage, lowering costs of goods sold, minimizing costs-to-serve, and optimizing the product mix, businesses can unlock significant opportunities for margin growth. Each of these strategies requires a thoughtful approach, leveraging both data-driven insights and operational improvements to ensure sustainable results.

Even small improvements in gross profit margins can have a transformative impact on overall profitability. As demonstrated, raising margins by just 1% can lead to a disproportionately large increase in operating earnings—fueling reinvestment, growth, and resilience.

Chapter 12
Organization and Culture

The quality of an organization is a critical element of long-term, sustained growth. Team members who feel appreciated, empowered, and respected will likely care more about the organization and be willing to go the extra mile to protect it and satisfy its customers. These are people who essentially "buy in" and are truly the "secret sauce" that can stimulate and maintain growth. This applies to all team member levels, whether the person is part or full time, hourly or salaried, in the field or the office, remote or in-person, or management or executive.

It is very common to hear leaders say, "Our people are our best asset." However, when they are asked how this came about, they frequently don't have a good answer. Without a very deliberate and focused approach, it is highly unlikely that your team will be significantly better than your competitors'.

Growth is facilitated by having the right people on the team in roles that optimize their satisfaction and contribution—and making your people truly your best asset is possible by focusing on improving:

- Team recruiting and/or selection.
- New team member onboarding by establishing a clear and defined onboarding process.
- Team member and/or manager training.

- Team member mentoring and/or coaching.
- The team member evaluation and professional development process.
- Your programs for the recognition and reward of key employees.
- Team member and manager succession planning and development and retention of key players.

Buy-In

Creating and maintaining manager and team buy-in unleashes an energized and motivated organization on your journey to success. Businesses with a culture that fosters engagement and alignment are more likely to pursue a common vision and fulfill their mission and are more resilient and flexible when facing adversity.

Businesses that demonstrate manager and team member buy-in generate energy, enthusiasm, creativity, and commitment, producing an intangible, highly valuable differentiator that facilitates success in the other Pillars of Growth. Managers and team members need to feel that they play key roles in the pursuit of success and that they genuinely matter in the plans and the outcomes for the business. (See Chapter 13 for more on buy-in.)

Engagement

Manager and team member engagement can propel growth significantly. Engagement and Buy-in are closely related. However, Buy-in is more about agreement and commitment to the company's overall vision and values, while engagement is about active involvement and emotional investment in daily work and organizational outcomes. Engagement impacts motivation, alignment with company goals, sense of ownership, innovation, productivity, and collaboration. The benefits can be enhanced customer satisfaction, reduced turnover costs, and a culture of adaptability that supports the smooth implementation of new strategies. Engaged employees are more likely to share ideas, embrace change, and deliver exceptional results, giving businesses a competitive edge and fostering long-term success. Simply put, investing in engagement isn't just about improving morale—it's a strategic imperative for sustained growth.

There are several elements to creating a high level of team engagement:

1. Clear and transparent communications are essential for engagement. Managers and team members should have a thorough understanding of:
   - The company's direction (Future State) or "where" the company is heading.
     - o "How" the company will transform from its Current State to the Future State.
     - o "Why" the Future State is believable and attainable.
     - o The company's progress towards achieving its Future State.

- Challenges and obstacles the company is experiencing—and how leadership plans to deal with them.

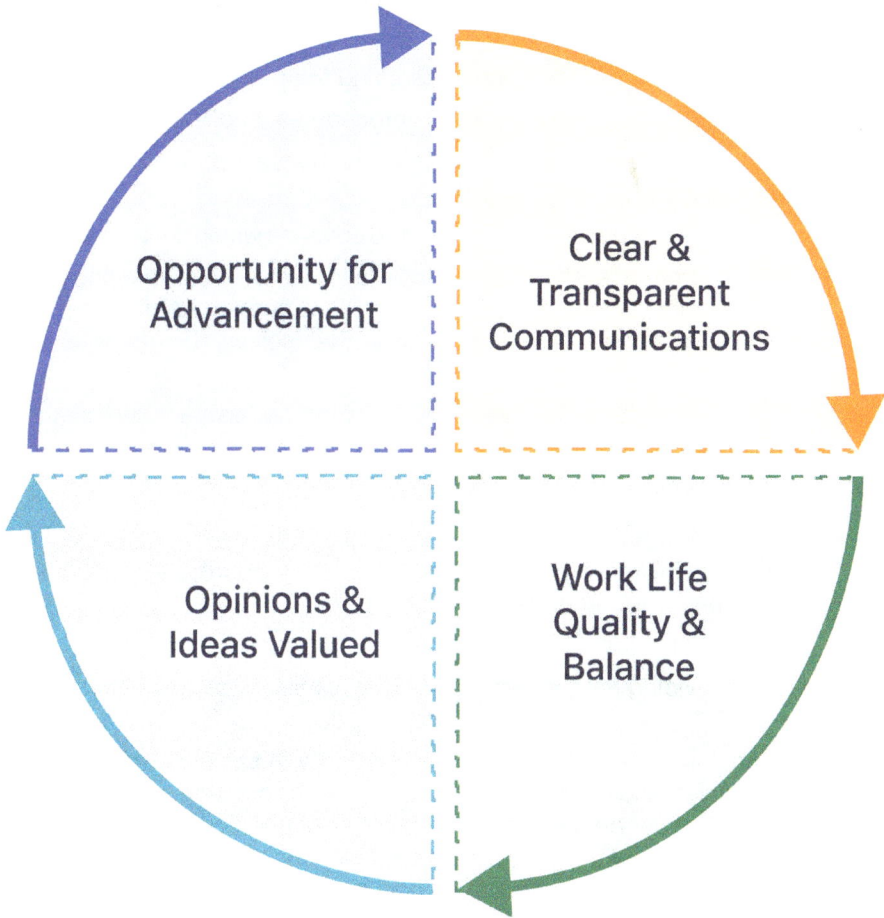

Opportunity for Advancement

Clear & Transparent Communications

Opinions & Ideas Valued

Work Life Quality & Balance

2. The quality of work life (the "environment") is also an important element of motivation and buy-in. Work life is impacted by:

- The physical work environment:
  - o Is the workplace clean and comfortable?
  - o Is the temperature reasonable and the air quality good?
  - o Is team safety at the location (inside and out) prioritized?
  - o Do managers and team members have the appropriate training, processes, equipment and tools, and supporting resources to be effective, reduce stress, and enhance job satisfaction?
  - o Is there privacy where necessary and appropriate?

- The culture—do team members believe that the company values respect, fairness, inclusion, work-life balance, engagement, and strong human resource practices? These can include:
  o Respectful treatment from managers, supervisors, and co-workers.
  o Feeling included, appreciated, and trusted.
  o Fair and consistent policies, procedures, and treatment.
  o Competitive and motivating compensation, incentives, and benefits.
  o Opportunities to learn, grow, and advance within the organization.
  o Appropriate work-life balance and flexibility—expecting team members to work hard but also allowing them to take paid time off, rest, and devote attention to themselves, their families, and their personal lives.
  o Ensuring team members are free from harassment, intimidation, and bullying.
  o Minimizing bureaucracy and office politics.
  o Having appropriate diversity and inclusion.
  o Offering managers and team members appropriate social and community engagement and activities.
  o Having clear lines of authority and responsibility.
  o Providing mental health and other similar support benefits.
- Balance—team members thrive when they feel the company genuinely understands and respects the importance of balancing work demands with personal life. This means creating an environment that allows people the time and flexibility to recharge, spend quality time with family, prioritize their health, and pursue personal passions, such as exercise, sports, and hobbies. By supporting this balance, businesses foster a healthier, more energized, and more engaged workforce.

3. Managers and team members should feel confident that their opinions and ideas are not only heard but also valued and thoughtfully considered. When employees believe their voices matter, it fosters a sense of inclusion, respect, and ownership in the company's mission. This environment encourages open dialogue, collaboration, and innovation, as individuals are more likely to share creative solutions and take initiative when they know their contributions are respected. Beyond just listening, it's important for leadership to demonstrate appreciation by acknowledging and acting on valuable input. This could mean implementing suggestions, providing constructive feedback, or simply recognizing contributions in meetings or performance reviews. When employees see their ideas making a tangible impact, it reinforces their

belief in the importance of their role and strengthens their connection to the organization's success.

4. Managers and team members must also trust that the company's growth and success will translate into **meaningful benefits** for them, such as opportunities for professional development, career advancement, or other forms of recognition—especially if those opportunities align with their personal goals and aspirations.

Example: Southwest Airlines' Employee-Centric Culture

Southwest Airlines is known for its employee-centric culture, which has contributed to its long-term success. The company built its business on the basis that happy employees lead to happy customers, and it invested heavily in employee training, development, and engagement. By creating a culture of empowerment and collaboration, Southwest built an engaged workforce and a loyal customer base.

Example: Microsoft's Transformation Under Satya Nadella

When Satya Nadella became CEO of Microsoft in 2014, he shifted the company's focus from a culture of internal competition to one of collaboration and empathy. This cultural shift empowered employees to innovate and contributed to Microsoft's resurgence as a leader in cloud computing and artificial intelligence.

Recruitment, Selection, Onboarding, and Training

A company's workforce can be its most vital asset and create a competitive advantage. Hiring the right people with the right skills, attitude, and growth potential lays the foundation for long-term success. Companies that have a reputation for being great places to work have an advantage in attracting people who align with their values, culture, and performance goals. Complement this with disciplined recruitment, selection, and development practices, and you can ensure that the organization is well-placed to create business success.

Effective onboarding and training allow new hires to adapt quickly, become productive sooner, and understand their role in contributing to the company's growth. Proper training ensures that they possess the skills and knowledge to perform at their best, reducing the time required to achieve operational efficiency.

Team members who feel appreciated, empowered, and respected will likely care more about the organization and be willing to go the extra mile to protect it and satisfy its customers. These are people who essentially "buy in" and are truly the "secret sauce" that can stimulate and maintain growth.

Recruiting the wrong people or failing to adequately onboard and train them can lead to high turnover, low morale, and wasted resources. Comprehensive recruitment and training strategies minimize these risks:

- Clearly defining job roles, responsibilities, and the related skill and experience requirements to do the job
- Using structured interviews, skills assessments, and behavioral tests to objectively evaluate candidates
- Ensuring consistency and reducing bias by involving multiple stakeholders in the decision-making process
- Assessing whether candidates align with the company's values and work environment
- Providing new hires with resources, schedules, and welcome messages before they officially start
- Creating a sense of belonging early with introductions to the team and company culture
- Holding orientation sessions that cover company history, mission, vision, values, and goals
- Assigning a mentor or buddy
- Defining short-term and long-term objectives for the new hire
- Creating ongoing training programs tailored to employee roles, career paths, and skill gaps

Conclusion

An organization's culture and structure are the foundation of sustainable growth. When businesses prioritize creating an environment where team members feel valued, respected, and empowered, they unlock a powerful force for innovation, productivity, and loyalty. The most successful organizations understand that their people are their greatest asset and invest in recruiting, developing, and retaining talent while fostering a culture of collaboration and trust.

Engaged employees drive customer satisfaction, reduce turnover, and propel the organization toward its goals. By focusing on clear communication, work-life balance, and the alignment of personal and organizational objectives, companies can create a workplace where team members are motivated to contribute their best efforts.

Organizational excellence and culture are not incidental to success—they are essential. Businesses that intentionally cultivate these elements will find themselves better positioned to achieve growth, overcome challenges, and thrive in an ever-changing marketplace.

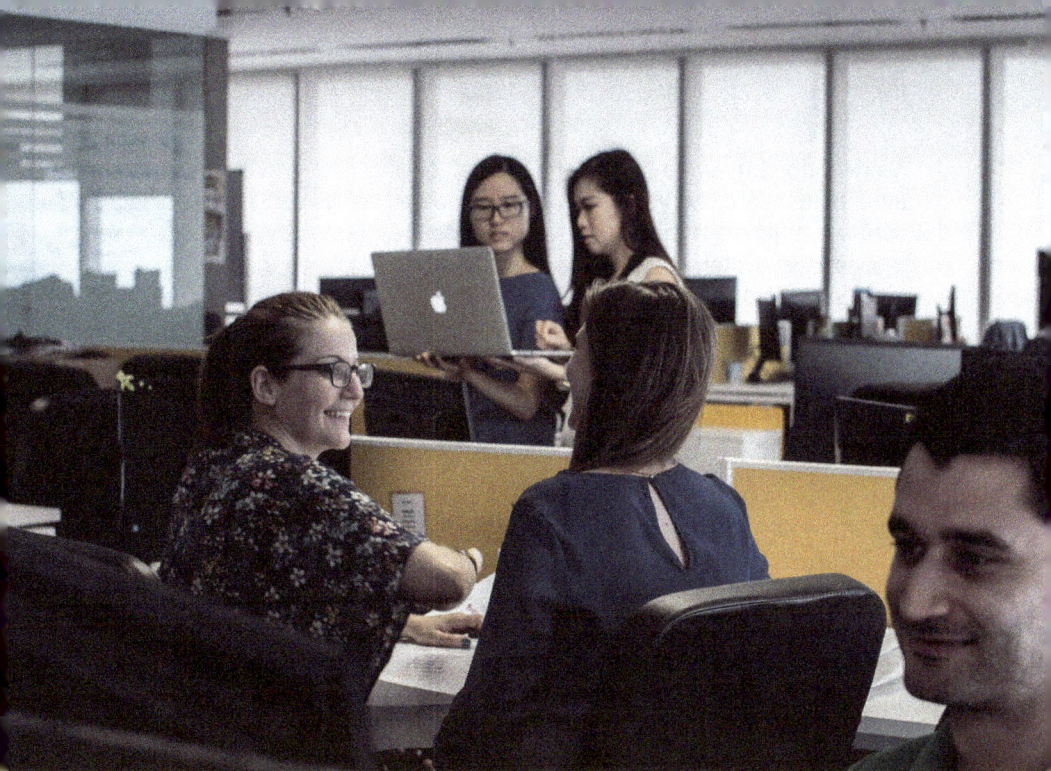

Chapter 13
Buy-In

Gaining buy-in from leaders, managers, and team members dramatically increases the likelihood of successfully executing your strategic growth plan. When all key team members are aligned on the fundamentals of the plan and committed to doing what it takes to implement its actions, your strategy is transformed from a mere blueprint into a powerful tool that lives in the organization and creates a far greater chance of delivering the desired results.

For a team to buy into a strategic growth plan, they generally need to understand "where" the company is heading, "what" it will take to get there, and "why" the plan is likely to work. This understanding is facilitated by "painting the picture" (as described in Chapter 5) and helps ensure the team's daily actions are in sync with the long-term goals of the business.

Secret Sauce

Few elements in a business are as valuable and impactful as manager and team member buy-in. This concept reflects the emotional and intellectual alignment of employees with the company's goals, vision, and values. It's not just about following directives—it's about fostering a deep commitment to the organization's success. When buy-in is achieved, team members take ownership and responsibility, driving elevated levels of engagement, motivation, productivity, trust, loyalty, passion, and creativity.

We describe buy-in as the "secret sauce" of business growth and success because of its intangible yet transformative power. It acts as the invisible force that connects leadership's vision with the team's actions. While strategies, processes, and systems are critical, their true impact depends on the people who execute them. A workforce with strong buy-in becomes unified, inspired, and innovative, creating a competitive edge that is not only formidable but also difficult to replicate or compete against.

Widespread Buy-In

Some business leaders hesitate to share the specifics of a growth plan, viewing it as sensitive information. Concerns often stem from fears that employees might feel the targets are unattainable or misinterpret the details. Team members may push for pay increases or, worse, leave the organization and share insights with competitors.

However, as with many business issues, the answer requires a thoughtful risk-reward analysis. In our experience, the benefits of transparency and alignment far outweigh the potential risks. Open communication fosters trust, builds engagement, and empowers teams to rally behind the company's vision. Still, every business must evaluate this balance based on its unique circumstances.

The level of detail shared can and should vary depending on the role. For example, the information you provide to a welder on the shop floor will differ from what you discuss with a department leader or executive. What matters is ensuring that every team member:

1. Understands the growth plan at a high level—its goals, purpose, and overall direction.
2. Feels valued and included in the process.
3. Knows how their role contributes directly to the plan's success.

When employees see the big picture and their part in it, they are more likely to commit to the organization's goals with focus and dedication. Managers lead with focus and conviction while team members execute with confidence and dedication, understanding how their efforts contribute to the organization reaching its goals. This shared commitment fuels accountability, innovation, and a sense of ownership, transforming the growth plan into a unified mission. The result is an energized organization moving cohesively toward success.

Without Buy-In

Now consider what happens when buy-in is absent. Without it, the execution of the plan is likely to become fragmented and disjointed. If managers and employees are unclear about the plan or how their roles fit into the bigger picture, they may disengage or prioritize tasks that do not align with strategic goals. Lack of commitment or even resistance to change often arises, as team members may view the plan as top-down rather than inclusive. This can lead to confusion, mistakes, delays, inefficiencies, and missed opportunities.

Even worse, a lack of buy-in may undermine morale. When managers or employees do not see the value in the plan or feel excluded from its creation, it can breed distrust and resentment. This disengagement not only jeopardizes the current strategy but can also have a long-term impact on company culture, making it harder to rally the team around future initiatives.

Buy-in is also critical during the inevitable challenges that accompany any growth effort. Plans rarely unfold perfectly, and unforeseen obstacles require agility and problem solving. Teams that have participated in creating the company's plans—and, as a result, have trust in its leadership—are more likely to rise to these challenges and collaborate to find solutions. Conversely, teams without buy-in may view challenges as further justification for their doubts, causing momentum to stall.

Communication

To ensure that managers and employees see the benefits of a strategic growth plan, businesses must prioritize clear and transparent communication and develop the benchmarks that will indicate progress (or the lack of progress) to help the team execute the strategy. Leaders should explain not just the goals of the plan but also the rationale behind it—why it is important, how it aligns with the company's values, and what success will look like. Targeted messaging is key—managers need to understand how the plan supports their leadership roles, while team members need to see how it positively impacts their day-to-day work and long-term career opportunities.

Transparency

Leadership transparency is essential to fostering buy-in because it builds trust, credibility, and a sense of shared purpose. When leaders are open about the reasons for the growth strategy, the challenges it addresses, and the risks involved, they show respect for their teams' intelligence and contributions. This honesty makes the strategy feel authentic rather than imposed, cultivating a stronger emotional connection to the plan.

Transparency also helps bridge the gap between high-level goals and individual roles. By sharing key metrics, progress updates, and even setbacks, leaders keep the team informed and engaged. This openness encourages collaboration, as employees are more likely to voice concerns, suggest improvements, and commit to the strategy when they feel fully informed.

Moreover, transparent leaders demonstrate accountability, setting an example that inspires managers and team members to take responsibility for their own roles and responsibilities in developing and executing the strategy. It transforms the growth plan from a top-down directive into a shared journey, where the group is invested in overcoming obstacles and achieving success.

Involvement and Engagement

Involvement is another critical factor. By engaging management and employees early in the process, seeking their input, and incorporating feedback, businesses can create a sense of ownership and demonstrate that the plan is not simply handed down but built collaboratively. Visualizing outcomes—such as highlighting specific growth opportunities, new markets, or professional development paths—makes the benefits tangible and relatable. Manager and employee involvement and engagement can also lead to new and better ideas and opportunities for growth and improvement.

Recognition and Rewards

Recognition also plays a role. Celebrating early wins tied to the plan can reinforce its value. Acknowledging individual and team contributions will help maintain engagement, alignment, and effort. Incentive plans that align manager, employee, and company success can also facilitate buy-in, business growth, and success.

If managers and employees are unclear about the plan or how their roles fit into the bigger picture, they may disengage or prioritize tasks that do not align with strategic goals. Lack of commitment or even resistance to change often arises, as team members may view the plan as top-down rather than inclusive.

Conclusion

Team buy-in can be the lifeblood of a successful strategic growth plan. It connects leadership's vision to the efforts of the entire organization, ensuring that the team is invested in shared success. Without it, the plan risks becoming just another document, gathering dust as the company struggles to achieve its potential.

Chapter 14
Leadership

Leadership is essential to the growth and success of virtually any venture. Consider how effective soldiers would be without their platoon leader, football players without their coach, or actors without their director. There is little difference in a business environment, and this is especially true for companies that plan to grow significantly.

It is often said, "It's lonely at the top." This is true. Leaders carry significant burdens and responsibilities that cannot be delegated. Invariably, there is unique pressure on the leader to execute the mission effectively, and the team looks to the leader for direction, inspiration, solutions, empathy, and strength. While leaders can be close and collegial with their team members, in times of need, when important decisions must be made, the leader is, indeed, alone. Advice can be sought, but ultimately, the buck does stop with the leader.

Five Key Elements

There are five key elements of a leader's role (we call these the Five Leadership Keys):

1. Develop and communicate a believable plan (strategist).
2. Select and train the team (coach).
3. Develop goals and standards and hold the team accountable for quality and results (manager).

4. Instill culture, collaboration, transparency, engagement, integrity, trust, motivation, team spirit, and loyalty (cheerleader).

5. Facilitate or direct course corrections when circumstances dictate (realist).

Like all people, leaders have good and bad days. While most people have the luxury of dealing with their ups and downs in relative obscurity, leaders are in the limelight most of the time. When a manager is told in front of his whole team that an essential machine has gone down, which is going to result in late deliveries to key customers, the team is going to witness in real-time how the manager reacts under stress. A manager who reacts calmly and methodically sends a very different message than one who yells and finger-points. How the leader reacts will have a significant impact on the culture and effectiveness of the team.

Stage Management

The reality is that the leader is like an actor on stage and the team is like the audience, observing the proceedings from a distance. Virtually every move the leader makes, including words, facial expressions, energy level, and body language, will be closely observed and taken in by the team and others. The best actors know how to seamlessly improvise when another actor forgets his or her lines or when a stagehand misplaces a prop in a manner that is unnoticeable to the audience. Similarly, great leaders exude poise and competence, even when things are not going according to plan.

A leader goes on stage in the parking lot and doesn't leave for the rest of the day. People will be watching. If an employee observes a leader who is smiling, looking confident, and exuding positive energy, they might deduce that things are going well in the company. Employees could come to a very different and potentially damaging conclusion if they see a leader who looks stressed, preoccupied, and worried.

Both employees and outside stakeholders (banks, suppliers, and customers) hold leaders to generally high standards. They expect leaders to excel in all the Five Leadership Keys described above and will enthusiastically follow and support leaders who do this. Conversely, they have little tolerance for failure. If the team loses confidence in the leader's ability to effectively execute the Five Leadership Keys, team effectiveness could rapidly deteriorate.

Leaders Are Still Human

Team members generally know that leaders are human, and they will overlook occasional minor shortcomings, especially if the leader demonstrates honesty, transparency, and humility. Even though standards for leaders are high, they are not expected to have all the answers. Team members will respect a leader who says, "I don't know, but I will find out!" or "I would like you and your teammates to help me figure out the right answer."

Leaders who demonstrate that they "go to bat" for the team and "have their back" generate a unique level of team spirit and loyalty (an important part of Key #4). Leaders can do this by giving team members appropriate recognition and rewards for their efforts and helping them through challenging times at work and home.

Know When to Step into the Wings

While leaders can be "on stage" a significant portion of the time, the very best leaders manage to step out of the limelight and into the wings as much as possible, empowering their teams to work together collaboratively to develop and implement the action plans to execute the leader's vision and even suggesting improvements or modifications to the vision.

By stepping aside, the leader allows team members to be creative and energized, frequently resulting in increased passion, commitment, and buy-in. In this environment, the leader moves from being the center of attention to a coach and cheerleader and only steps in when guidance is needed and acknowledgment or recognition is warranted.

Leadership Skills Can Be Learned

A few people naturally excel at all Five Leadership Keys and become great leaders. However, many great leaders learn and enhance these skills as their careers develop. Leadership coaching, training, and practice can help leaders significantly enhance these skills. Regular team member engagement and satisfaction surveys, coupled with appropriate questions about leadership effectiveness, can provide valuable benchmarking and feedback about leaders' progress and development.

Character and Competence

Leadership credibility, integrity, competence, and style are huge drivers of team buy-in and successfully executing your business's growth plans.

Perceived character and competence are key elements in attracting and retaining the talent needed to succeed.

- Do you care about your team?
- Can you be trusted to be straight with your team?
- Do you treat people fairly and consistently?
- Have you established appropriate values and norms?
- Have you hired competent people and assigned them to roles that are a good fit for their skills and personalities?
- Are you committed to excellence?
- Do you appreciate, acknowledge, and recognize the contributions of managers and team members?
- Do you hold underperformers accountable?

- Do you hold yourself accountable?
- Do you have empathy and compassion?
- Do you listen?
- Are you a "servant leader" or a "command-and-control manager"?
- Are you a worthy and competent leader with a plan for success?
- Do you make decisions in a logical, consistent, and data-driven manner?
- How do you react under pressure or during a crisis?

Leadership is a responsibility. Good leaders feel accountable to their teams. The team counts on leadership to provide realistic targets and also the resources to achieve both the business's and their own professional goals. They want to believe in you, but it is your responsibility to show them you are up to the task. It is virtually impossible to have strong buy-in without capable leadership.

The reality is that the leader is like an actor on stage and the team is like the audience, observing the proceedings from a distance. Virtually every move the leader makes, including words, facial expressions, energy level, and body language, will be closely observed and taken in by the team and others.

Conclusion

Leadership is the cornerstone of a business's growth and success. A strong leader inspires, directs, and empowers their team while shouldering the ultimate responsibility for decisions and outcomes. By mastering the Five Leadership Keys—strategist, coach, manager, cheerleader, and realist—leaders can build trust, foster engagement, and drive results.

Leadership is not about being perfect but about being authentic, empathetic, and committed to the success of the team and the organization. Great leaders set the example, demonstrating accountability, resilience, and the ability to adapt under pressure. They also know when to step into the wings, empowering their teams to innovate and collaborate.

Leadership is a continuous journey, and businesses that prioritize strong, capable leaders will find themselves better positioned to achieve and sustain success.

Chapter 15
Power of Teamwork

Consistently achieving business growth is most effectively attained when the plans are developed and implemented in a team-based manner. This is built on the SOAR principles that organization and culture are key fundamentals to success. This approach provides multiple benefits:

1. In most situations, when trying to develop ideas or solve problems, a group of people is more likely to generate a broader array of creative options than one person. "More heads are better than one" is especially true if the members of the group have diverse roles, backgrounds, and experiences AND the group is able to accept challenges to the status quo and distill worthwhile ideas into possible Opportunities and Necessities.

2. Team members can help others understand and discuss issues from different perspectives that might not have been previously apparent to them individually.

3. Team members feed off each other. One team member may propose an idea that triggers another team member to generate a different or better idea.

4. Team members who have participated in developing ideas will feel stronger ownership of and commitment to successful implementation.

5. Working as a team can build relationships and trust that didn't exist before.

6. Communications are improved because more people are "in the room" when decisions are made, as opposed to them hearing about it in a memo from the CEO or other leader.

7. Team members learn how to collaborate and resolve conflicts.

Example: Google

Cross-functional collaboration across teams is a hallmark of Google's work culture. Engineers, product managers, designers, and marketers collaborate closely to develop new products and features. Google's ability to foster teamwork led to the creation of innovative products like Google Maps, Gmail, and Android. For example, Google Maps was developed as part of a collaboration between acquired startups and Google's internal teams, which allowed them to quickly scale and launch a product that transformed the way people navigate.

Example: Pixar

Pixar's "Braintrust" meetings bring together a group of directors, writers, and producers to collaborate on every movie. These sessions focus on open, honest feedback, where all ideas are shared and improved upon collectively. Pixar's collaborative culture, combined with an uncompromising approach to providing consistent quality, has led to an unparalleled run of successful animated films, from *Toy Story* to *Finding Nemo* to *Coco*. Each movie is the result of intense teamwork and cross-departmental collaboration among animators, scriptwriters, and technical staff.

On the value of a team, Ed Catmull, a founder and president of Pixar, has said, "If you give a good idea to a mediocre team, they'll screw it up. But if you give a mediocre idea to a great team, they'll make it work."

Teamwork is the force multiplier that transforms individual efforts into collective success.

Conclusion

Teamwork is the force multiplier that transforms individual efforts into collective success. By fostering collaboration, communication, and trust, businesses unlock a wealth of creativity, innovation, and problem-solving capability. A team-based approach not only generates more diverse and effective ideas but also builds stronger ownership and commitment to their execution.

When diverse perspectives come together in a culture of openness and mutual respect, even the most complex challenges can be overcome, and extraordinary results can be achieved. No single person can drive growth alone—success is a collective endeavor. By nurturing teamwork and creating an environment where collaboration thrives, businesses can achieve their goals more efficiently and effectively, building a foundation for lasting growth and innovation.

Chapter 16

Accounting, Finance, and Technology

Accounting and Information

Good information enables growth. Informed decisions are the foundation of successful business growth.

At SOAR, we define "good information" as a combination of:

1. Accurate, timely data.

2. Clear, actionable presentation.

   When data is relevant and presented in a user-friendly format, it transforms into a powerful tool for decision-making. Add a culture of open discussion grounded in facts and constructive opinions, and you have the ideal environment for sound decision-making and effective risk management.

   Businesses need good information for multiple reasons, including that it allows them to provide:

   - Performance reports: Updates and reports about the company's performance and results to lenders, regulatory and tax authorities, shareholders, and other stakeholders. This information is often historical and not provided on a real-time basis, but it may include forecasts and estimates of future performance. The degree of detail is dependent on the requirements of the audience and can vary from granular to highly summarized.

- Operational decision-making: Reports and dashboards to leaders, managers, and team members to enable the business to manage risk and choose appropriate courses of action to execute the company's plans cost-effectively. This information may be detailed, granular, or summarized, but a common element is that it is of more value the closer to real-time the information becomes available.

Imagine playing a football or basketball game without a scoreboard that tells players, coaches, and officials the score, the number of timeouts remaining, or the length of time left to play. This would likely have a serious detrimental impact on the ability of players and coaches to maximize their performance. Similarly, businesses need dynamic scoreboards that facilitate informed and optimal decisions quickly enough to respond to the company's particular challenges or opportunities.

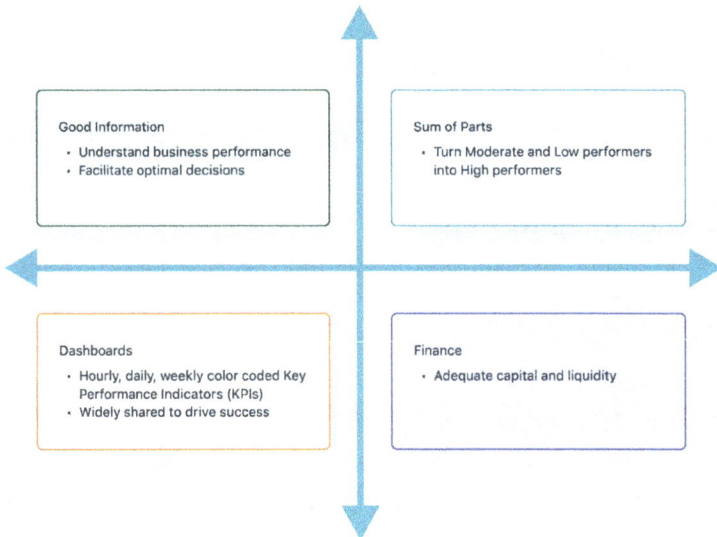

Good Information
- Understand business performance
- Facilitate optimal decisions

Sum of Parts
- Turn Moderate and Low performers into High performers

Dashboards
- Hourly, daily, weekly color coded Key Performance Indicators (KPIs)
- Widely shared to drive success

Finance
- Adequate capital and liquidity

Timely Information

Leaders, managers, and team members make multiple decisions every day. These range from pricing a product or service, scheduling work, negotiating the purchase of raw materials, and hiring new team members to buying new machinery, developing a new product line, entering a new market or acquiring a competitor. The ability to make the most favorable decisions will be significantly impacted by the quality, accuracy, and timeliness of information available to the business.

The timeliness of information is critical. The quicker you learn that you have a quality problem, for example, the better your ability to identify the root causes and take corrective action.

Types of Information Needed

- Financial insight—accurate revenues, expenses, and profitability by division, business unit, product line, product, region, market, segment, customer, and salesperson.

- Trends and patterns—which parts of the business are growing, declining, erratic, or seasonal.

- Budgets, forecasts, and goals—to both develop targets and desired outcomes for the business and then to compare actual results to expectations.

- Productivity metrics—understanding which machines, technology, teams, and functions are performing to standards and expectations.

- Quality, errors, scrap, and rework—understanding where work is not being done correctly the first time, triggering waste and inefficiency.

- Asset management efficiency—collection of accounts receivable, inventory turnover, and equipment and people utilization.

- Return on Investment—how productive spending on marketing, equipment, technology, or additional human resources has been.

Businesses need dynamic scoreboards that facilitate informed and optimal decisions quickly enough to respond to the company's particular challenges or opportunities.

Team Performance Information

Good information also pertains to the performance of team members throughout the organization, from the CEO to a part-time employee or even a consultant. Understanding who the high, moderate, and low performers are and creating pathways to upgrade the organization is a key strength of growth-minded companies.

Relevant team member surveys, individual and group evaluations, and safety and productivity reports all provide information on the quality of an organization and how well it is executing its plans.

Training, technology, feedback and coaching programs, and incentive payment initiatives are solutions that can resolve the issues identified.

Example: Apple's Strong Cash Management and Strategic Investments

Apple is renowned for its meticulous financial planning and cash management. One of the key factors behind Apple's consistent growth is its focus on maintaining a strong cash position. With billions in cash reserves, Apple has had the flexibility to invest in R&D, acquire strategic assets, and expand its product offerings while maintaining a high level of liquidity.

Example: WeWork's Overexpansion

WeWork, the shared office space company, expanded aggressively without maintaining sound financial controls. The company signed long-term leases for hundreds of office spaces, but its revenue did not keep pace with its growing expenses. As a result, WeWork faced a liquidity crisis and had to scale back its operations dramatically. This is a clear example of how poor financial planning can derail a company's growth.

The Sum of the Parts—Unlocking Granular Insights

Most businesses are an accumulation of many smaller parts or mini businesses, each contributing uniquely to the whole. Every product line, market segment, geographic region, distribution channel, and technology—or even large customers—can be thought of as mini-businesses within the larger business.

Analyzing and understanding the performance of the individual parts will drive insights into strategies that can improve the overall business. Looking exclusively at consolidated results misses out on the valuable information that can be gained from a granular examination.

Most businesses are an accumulation of many smaller parts or mini businesses, each contributing uniquely to the whole.

By understanding and optimizing each mini-business, organizations can elevate the performance of the whole. This granular approach not only drives operational and strategic excellence but also enhances resilience and adaptability in an ever-changing market landscape. The true strength of any business lies in the sum of its parts. By analyzing and improving these individual components, companies can unlock their full potential and achieve lasting success.

A more granular approach allows the business to:

- Recognize which product lines, segments, channels, technologies, customer groups, or regions are driving the bulk of revenue and profitability. This helps allocate resources to areas with the highest potential for growth or return on investment.

- Highlight underperforming segments that may require corrective action, such as a shift in strategy, cost reduction, or even divestment.

- Determine which low performers can be turned into moderate or high performers.

- Accept that some low performers might be important to keep for strategic reasons—but do not forget that they are still low performers. For example, a low-performing product or region may be important to retaining a relationship with a key customer.

- Drive accountability. When individual components are tracked and measured, teams and managers are more accountable for the performance of their respective areas, fostering a culture of ownership and continuous improvement.

Example: General Electric

General Electric (GE), once a sprawling conglomerate, faced significant challenges in maintaining profitability across its wide range of businesses. Under CEO Larry Culp, GE embarked on a major restructuring plan, which involved selling or spinning off several underperforming divisions to focus on its core strengths in aviation, power, and healthcare. GE sold its financial arm, GE Capital, which had been a major drag on the company's performance following the 2008 financial crisis. It also sold its lighting, appliance, and healthcare divisions. By shedding these non-core assets, GE has been able to reduce debt and refocus on its core businesses, leading to improved financial performance.

Example: eBay

eBay is another example of a company that improved its financial performance by divesting non-core business units. In 2015, eBay spun off its payments arm, PayPal, into a separate publicly traded company. While PayPal was highly successful, it was growing in a different direction from eBay's core e-commerce business. The separation allowed PayPal to grow independently, and it became one of the leading digital payment platforms globally. For eBay, shedding PayPal enabled the company to focus on improving its marketplace operations without the distraction of managing two very different businesses. The spin-off allowed both companies to thrive independently.

Using Dashboards

While the standard method of communicating financial information is traditionally monthly financial statements, dashboards, which communicate actual results compared to goals for key performance indicators (KPIs) or metrics and are made available to managers and team members on a daily or weekly basis—or even on an hourly or real-time basis—are useful tools in overseeing the business and gauging how well it is executing its plans.

Dashboards often combine data with charts, graphs, or color-coded indicators. Green represents results that are performing at or ahead of goals, red shows underperforming areas, and yellow reflects areas performing close to goals and that may require attention to avoid slipping into the red or helping them move up into green.

KPIs should be selected based on their priority relative to the company achieving its plans. It is easy for a business to track too many initiatives and become bogged down in detail. The chief value of dashboards is that they communicate to leaders, managers and team members in a highly efficient manner whether the company, business unit, or product is on track to achieve its goals. KPIs should evolve as the business does. What was relevant 12 or 24 months ago may not be as relevant today.

The ultimate goal of dashboards and KPIs is to help managers and team members understand if they are doing what it takes for the company to achieve its goals. If they can tell if they had a "good day" (and week and month), it will provide the company with a significantly greater chance of succeeding.

Example: Google

Google's teams use dashboards extensively for various metrics, including website performance, advertising revenue, and server uptime. Real-time data helps employees monitor performance and optimize services immediately. Google focuses on KPIs like user engagement, ad click-through rates, server performance, and product adoption rates. Each department uses customized dashboards to track metrics relevant to its goals.

Finance

Cash is the lifeblood of any business, enabling growth, stability, and resilience. Adequate capital and liquidity are essential for funding operations, working capital, marketing efforts, equipment, real estate, and team development. Growth requires not only investment but also a financial cushion to navigate unexpected challenges and economic downturns.

To ensure adequate cash flow and a financial cushion, businesses must develop accurate and realistic forecasts. Effective financial projections help businesses:

- Anticipate Cash Needs: Identify the funds required to meet both short-term obligations and long-term growth objectives.
- Manage Contingencies: Prepare for unexpected events, such as market disruptions, operational issues, or economic downturns.
- Enhance Decision Making: Provide clarity on whether to prioritize internal reinvestment, secure loans, or seek external equity financing.
- Build Stakeholder Confidence: Reassure lenders, investors, and other stakeholders about the business's stability and future prospects by using realistic, transparent, flexible, and data-driven projections.

Best practices for accurate forecasting include:

- Regular Updates: Projections should be revised frequently to reflect changing market conditions and operational realities.
- Scenario Planning: Incorporate optimistic, realistic, and pessimistic scenarios to prepare for various outcomes.
- Include Contingencies: Allocate funds for unexpected expenses to avoid a cash flow crisis.
- Engage Stakeholders: Involve managers and key team members in the forecasting process for diverse perspectives and buy-in.

There are multiple potential sources of cash:

- Earnings available for reinvestment.
- Investors who will own part of the business.
- Sale of surplus or unnecessary assets.
- Owners' personal savings.
- Money borrowed from friends and family.
- Third-party financing, such as loans from banks and other institutions.

It is generally more difficult and more expensive for start-ups and underperforming businesses to access funding without additional collateral or guarantees from parties with strong financial positions.

Securing capital comes with trade-offs. Third-party financing will have different costs, terms, requirements, and conditions associated with them:

- Borrowed money usually requires regular interest payments.
  - o Loans may also require regular repayment of the principal amount.
  - o Some of these loans might need to be secured by assets of the business.
  - o Frequently, personal guarantees by the company owners are required.
  - o Banks and lenders also can charge fees and impose "covenants" (which are performance requirements for the business). If the business does not comply with these requirements, the lender might be able to accelerate the loan and/or charge higher interest rates and fees.
- Investments by parties that then become equity holders might be less onerous in the short term in that they usually do not require interest or principal payments. However, in the long term, they are often more expensive than borrowed money because of the ownership dilution.

Businesses need to try to balance the cost, terms, and availability of funds with Opportunities and Necessities to meet their plans. As explained above, in many cases, there will be a "price" to be paid for this help. Some of this may be in cash and some in "equity." If you are starting a business, you may have to dig into your savings or seek funding from friends and family, and this may involve giving up a "piece of the action." If you are an established business, you may need to reinvest earnings, obtain additional loans, or bring in investors. This may help expand the business and lead to a bigger long-term value, but it will cost you in the short term.

Almost every successful entrepreneur who wants to scale their business knows they will need to deal with the possibility that they will not end up owning 100% of the enterprise. To be successful, they might have to give up some ownership to attract the right talent, resources, partners, funders, and investors.

The goal should be to build a great business that creates value for all the parties that contribute to success. Significant but still partial ownership of a larger, more diverse and stable company may be worth the tradeoff.

While obtaining the most funds at the lowest cost is desirable, practical realities usually dictate a trade-off to ensure that the business has access to the funds it needs.

Example: Airbnb's Financing for Growth and Strategic Resilience

Airbnb relied heavily on equity financing during its early stages to grow its platform and expand globally. The company raised billions in multiple funding rounds from venture capital firms, which allowed it to invest in technology, build its brand, and enter new markets.

When the COVID-19 pandemic hit, Airbnb's business was severely impacted. To weather the storm, Airbnb raised an additional $2 billion through equity and debt financing. The company later went public through a highly successful IPO in 2020, raising $3.5 billion.

Businesses need to try to balance the cost, terms, and availability of funds with Opportunities and Necessities to meet their plans. While obtaining the most funds at the lowest cost is desirable, practical realities usually dictate a trade-off to ensure that the business has access to the funds it needs.

Conclusion

In today's dynamic business environment, success hinges on the ability to make informed decisions, manage resources effectively, and adapt to challenges with agility.

Accounting, finance, and technology are the pillars that support informed decision-making, effective risk management, and sustainable business growth. Accurate, timely, and actionable information allows businesses to make strategic choices, respond quickly to challenges, and seize new opportunities. Dashboards and KPIs provide leaders with the clarity needed to track progress, measure success, and adjust plans to stay on course. Granular insight into the performance of individual business components frequently reveals opportunities for growth in profitability.

Financial stability is equally critical. Sound cash management, realistic forecasting, and a strategic approach to securing capital ensure that businesses have the resources to grow and be responsive—not reactive—to unexpected disruptions. Ultimately, the ability to integrate accounting, finance, and technology into a cohesive framework empowers businesses to unlock their full potential.

Chapter 17

Responsiveness and Execution

"Responsiveness and execution" refers to how successfully your business produces and brings your products and services to market—and how successfully it creates long-lasting and profitable relationships with customers, suppliers, and internal and external stakeholders.

Responsiveness

Creating consistently high levels of customer satisfaction is a significant catalyst for growth.

Unless you have a monopoly or highly desirable and unique product that is not available elsewhere, customers usually have options and choices about who they buy from. You not only want them to keep buying your current offering, but you also want them to be open to purchasing new products and services. Ultimately, you want them to become advocates for your business and your brands. Customer satisfaction is enhanced by:

1. Providing the customer with a compelling value proposition—products and services that offer significant value and satisfaction—creating a better overall experience than other alternatives (see additional comments in Chapter 10).

2. Anticipating and being highly responsive to customer needs. This is sometimes referred to as providing the optimal "customer journey."

Being highly responsive to customer needs includes:

- Strengthening commitment to—and actions for—customer satisfaction.
- Reducing out-of-stock inventory.
- Improving on-time delivery and/or fill rates.
- Reducing customer lead times and response times.
- Improving response speed and quality of information when dealing with customer questions or complaints.
- Improving policies, rules, practices, and/or systems to make it easier and more efficient for customers to do business with the company.
- Developing a continuous "feedback loop" to ensure the company is at least meeting and often exceeding customer expectations. This needs to be based on true "arm's length" criteria, and corrective actions (including training and policy changes) need to be a core tenet of the business.

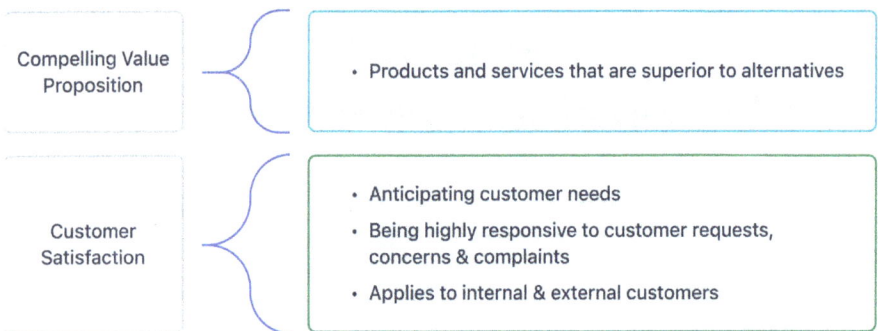

Compelling Value Proposition	• Products and services that are superior to alternatives
Customer Satisfaction	• Anticipating customer needs • Being highly responsive to customer requests, concerns & complaints • Applies to internal & external customers

Being highly responsive to customer needs can be a significant contributor to customer loyalty. While satisfying customer needs can have a short-term cost, the longer-term benefits derived from satisfied customers are generally very valuable. Satisfied customers are more likely to recommend your business or provide positive online reviews. Satisfied customers also promote increased efficiency and improved team morale. Dealing with irate customers can take a huge toll on staff productivity and job satisfaction, which can have a negative impact on growth.

And remember—customers exist both externally and internally.

- The salesperson who worked extremely hard to receive an order only to see it arrive late, incomplete, or, worse, with a quality issue loses faith in the business.

- The customer service agent who is trying to provide accurate information and does not receive a timely or precise response from a colleague can become frustrated and unmotivated.
- The production manager who cannot receive supplies because an invoice has not been paid and communication has been lacking will be angry and discouraged.

Successful businesses foster a culture of accountability and reward actions that improve customer satisfaction inside and outside of the business. This builds trust throughout the organization and improves team morale and engagement.

While several well-known companies built their reputations for customer service in the direct-to-consumer world (Amazon, Nordstrom, Zappos), many industrial and commercial businesses rely on their reputations to also attract both team members and suppliers. Companies as diverse as Wegmans Food Markets, Hilton Hotels, American Express, and David Weekley Homes all use their presence on Fortune's list of "100 Best Companies to Work For" as a way to build their reputations.

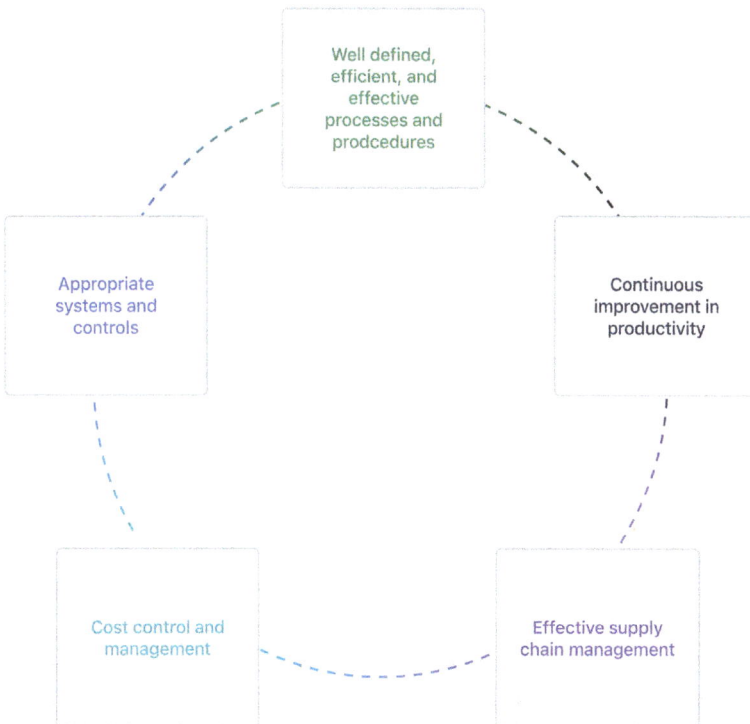

Well defined, efficient, and effective processes and prodcedures

Appropriate systems and controls

Continuous improvement in productivity

Cost control and management

Effective supply chain management

Example: Domino's

After receiving negative feedback about the taste of its pizza, Domino's responded by completely overhauling its pizza recipe and being transparent with its customers about the changes. Domino's also introduced innovative features like the Pizza Tracker, which allows customers to track their orders in real-time, and improved its delivery technology to reduce wait times. It also expanded into new delivery formats, such as autonomous vehicles and drone delivery, to meet customer expectations for faster, more reliable service. Domino's responsiveness to customer feedback led to a dramatic turnaround, making it one of the top pizza chains in the world.

Creating consistently high levels of customer satisfaction is a significant catalyst for growth.

Execution

Efficient and effective operational execution provides critical foundations for growth. Without consistent and proficient operational execution, it is extremely difficult to maintain a high level of overall business growth and ongoing customer satisfaction.

Strong operational execution includes:

- Well-defined, efficient, and effective processes and procedures
  - o Standard operating procedures.
  - o Appropriate processes, systems, and controls.
  - o Comprehensive quality assurance processes, systems, controls, and responses to issues.
  - o Effective health and safety policies, procedures, and practices.
- Continuous improvement in productivity
  - o Efficient and effective utilization of materials, people, and equipment.
  - o Relevant products and services that both satisfy market demand and minimize waste and obsolescence.
  - o Consistent high levels of product and service quality, minimizing rework and duplication of effort (as well as meeting customer expectations).
  - o Accurate, timely, reliable, and effective information that is appropriately used.
  - o Well-maintained equipment that uses up-to-date (and, ideally, state-of-the-art) technology.

o Eliminating inefficiencies, bottlenecks, and capacity constraints in all significant processes.

o Continuous improvement and/or Lean/Six Sigma programs.

o Where applicable and practical, improving productivity via automation, robotics, artificial intelligence, improved training, reduced rework, and the reduction/elimination of duplication of effort and/or unnecessary activities.

o Reducing material and/or product costs via lowering scrap rates, reducing obsolescence, improving material yields, and avoiding product rework.

o Using "gainsharing," "piecework," or other incentive systems to encourage and motivate team members to help the company improve its operation execution and efficiency.

Example: Toyota's Focus on Execution

Toyota's commitment to execution through its "lean manufacturing" system has made it one of the most efficient car manufacturers in the world. By eliminating waste, improving processes, and focusing on continuous improvement, Toyota has been able to maintain its competitive edge and grow consistently.

- Effective supply chain management

o Enhancing scheduling systems' effectiveness and user-friendliness.

o Focusing on warehousing, distribution, shipping, and logistics to reduce overall shipping and handling costs and in-transit times to improve speed to market and accuracy of inventories.

o Improving supply chain management and purchasing to create a responsive supply network that will optimize and balance working capital availability, lead times and minimum order quantities, cost management, and quality assurance.

o Using vendor-consigned inventory (where vendors supply inventory to the company, but the company is not invoiced for the inventory until the company uses it) or vendor-managed inventory (where vendors supply inventory on consignment, but the vendor also manages inventory levels and replenishment).

o Developing relationships with suppliers to obtain flexible payment terms that allow the business to react to business cycles and external events that negatively affect cash flow.

Example: Walmart's Use of Supply Chain as a Competitive Advantage

Walmart is widely recognized for having one of the most efficient supply chains in the world, which has been key to its success and dominance in the retail sector. The company has invested heavily in technology and logistics to optimize its supply chain, enabling it to offer low prices and a vast range of products. Walmart's supply chain uses a vendor-managed inventory (VMI) system that allows suppliers to monitor the retailer's inventory levels and replenish stock automatically, reducing the need for Walmart to hold large inventories. The company also uses advanced data analytics to forecast demand and optimize the movement of goods from warehouses to stores. Walmart's supply chain efficiency enables it to keep costs low while offering a wide product selection, driving its growth to become one of the largest retailers in the world.

- Creating a cost-effective business environment
    - o Reducing costs via better purchasing and/or obtaining regular/ multiple price quotes from key vendors, improved budgeting and cost controls, or centralization of operations or other similar actions.
    - o Reducing selling, general, and administrative costs in a targeted manner, which results in the business having less fixed costs without impairing growth opportunities.
    - o Implementing sustainability measures to improve the company's total impact and reputation and, at the same time, benefit from state and federal tax and other subsidies.
    - o Regularly analyzing all expenditures and questioning whether expenses are essential.
    - o Benchmarking the company's costs against other companies in the industry or similar industries.
    - o Exploring ways to reduce the company's physical footprint to increase efficiency and/or reduce occupancy and other costs.
    - o Exploring ways to move to lower-cost locations to reduce occupancy, logistics, and other costs—if such moves would not disrupt operations or impact customer satisfaction.
    - o Exploring ways to reduce energy costs via new lighting, energy controls, solar, and wind.
    - o Exploring customer self-service via automated attendants, portals, self-checkout, and chat technology.
    - o Reducing the business's "physical footprint" by using contractors, selling underutilized equipment, outsourcing functions, disposing of obsolete inventories and materials, and decreasing leased or owned space that is not being efficiently used.
    - o Upgrading the team through better hiring, training, improved technology or other resources, and performance management programs.

o Outsourcing can also offer cost savings opportunities. By shifting certain tasks to outside resources or lower-cost regions or countries, the business can access lower-cost providers or move certain functions to a variable rather than fixed cost. Successfully taking advantage of outsourcing may mean the business needs to invest to ensure that the quality and timeliness of the source meet the company's standards.

Example: General Motors's Restructuring and Cost Cuts

General Motors faced a severe financial crisis during the 2008 economic downturn, ultimately filing for bankruptcy. To return to profitability, GM embarked on an aggressive cost-cutting strategy as part of its restructuring plan. This included closing underperforming plants, reducing the number of brands (such as discontinuing Pontiac, Saturn, and Hummer), and cutting jobs. The company also renegotiated labor contracts with unions to reduce pension and healthcare liabilities. GM emerged from bankruptcy in 2009 as a more efficient and financially sound company. The restructuring allowed GM to reduce costs significantly and return to profitability, paving the way for its resurgence as one of the leading global automakers.

Example: Airbus's Lean Manufacturing and Supply Chain Optimization

Airbus, the European aerospace manufacturer, faced cost overruns and delays in its A380 and A350 XWB programs, which put pressure on its financial performance. To address these challenges, Airbus launched its Power8 restructuring program, which focused on cost reduction and operational efficiencies. The program included consolidating production facilities, reducing supplier costs, and improving lean manufacturing processes. Airbus also optimized its supply chain by negotiating better terms with suppliers and reducing waste throughout the production process. The cost savings helped Airbus achieve stronger financial performance and increase its market share in the commercial aircraft industry.

Without consistent and proficient operational execution, it is extremely difficult to maintain a high level of overall business growth and ongoing customer satisfaction.

Example: Procter & Gamble's Zero-Based Budgeting

Procter & Gamble (P&G), one of the world's largest consumer goods companies, implemented zero-based budgeting (ZBB) to improve its cost structure. Under ZBB, every expense must be justified for each new period rather than simply adjusting the previous year's budget. This forced managers to scrutinize spending and eliminate inefficiencies across the organization. P&G also reduced the number of product variants and brands in its portfolio, cutting down on complexity and production costs. The company sold off non-core brands, such as Duracell, and focused on its core brands, like Tide, Pampers, and Gillette. P&G's cost-cutting measures allowed it to improve profitability while freeing up resources to reinvest in innovation, marketing, and growth for its core brands.

Systems and Controls

The appropriate controls, systems, and processes that help ensure that the business is managing operations and risks effectively are vital to creating a resilient and stable business environment. This is another key attribute of successful growth-minded companies, regardless of business size and maturity.

These include:

- Standard operating procedures.
- Quality procedures, processes, and controls.
- Safety policies and procedures.
- Internal controls.
- Risk management controls.
- Environmental controls.
- Information systems and cybersecurity and controls.
- R&D and innovation controls
- Evaluation of future spending and investment plans and reviews of past performance and decision-making.

Example: Toyota Motor Corporation

Toyota is renowned for its Toyota Production System, which emphasizes lean manufacturing and continuous improvement (including Kaizen). Their rigorous standard operating procedures and quality controls have set industry benchmarks for efficiency and product quality.

Conclusion

Responsiveness and execution are the twin engines of business growth and customer satisfaction. A business that excels in both areas creates lasting value, builds strong customer loyalty, and enhances operational efficiency. Responsiveness ensures that customers feel heard, valued, and prioritized, fostering long-term relationships and advocacy. Execution transforms strategy into reality, delivering consistent quality, efficiency, and reliability that meet and exceed customer expectations.

By focusing on improving processes, optimizing supply chains, managing costs, and leveraging innovative systems, businesses position themselves to thrive in competitive markets. Companies that combine a relentless focus on customer satisfaction with world-class operational execution will stand out. Sustainable growth requires not just strategic vision but also disciplined execution and adaptability to meet evolving customer and market demands.

Chapter 18
Pivoting

In today's dynamic business environment, the ability to pivot and adapt is very important. Markets are constantly evolving due to technological advancements, shifts in consumer preferences, regulatory changes, economic fluctuations, and competitive innovation.

Businesses that fail to adapt risk irrelevance and, ultimately, obsolescence. It is crucial for businesses to be willing and able to pivot and adapt their strategies in response to changing conditions.

Examples:

Retail companies from Blockbuster to Kmart to Circuit City failed to pivot when technology and the competition evolved to tap into changing consumer preferences, leading to their decline and subsequent elimination.

Adaptability allows a business to identify and capitalize on new opportunities, whether that means targeting a new customer base, shifting the way they deliver products and services, launching new products, or entering a new market.

During crises, such as economic downturns or global pandemics, businesses that can pivot are more likely to weather the storm. Companies that are too rigid can collapse under the pressure. This includes being willing to manage expenses and work with suppliers, customers, investors, and financial institutions to create liquidity and ensure that the business can not only survive but emerge in a strong position once business conditions moderate.

Example:

During the COVID-19 pandemic, many restaurants pivoted to focus on outdoor dining, takeout, delivery, and meal kits when dine-in services were restricted.

Customer preferences and behaviors evolve over time. Being able to pivot allows businesses to respond quickly to changing demands, keeping them relevant to their customer base.

Example:

During the pandemic, Starbucks shifted its business model to prioritize mobile ordering and drive-thru services, which became essential as foot traffic declined. The company's rapid pivot helped sustain revenue. However, as consumers began returning to in-store shopping, they found that the shift to a less personal arrangement, with the preference given to "call ahead" customers, along with increased pricing, diminished the experience they were seeking. They preferred their "relationship" with a barista and the store being their hangout. As a result, Starbucks has been losing customers and is on its third CEO in five years. This is an example of the SOAR philosophy that strategies and plans need regular reviews and evaluations to ensure that they remain relevant in the current marketplace.

Businesses that can pivot faster than competitors often gain a competitive edge. Flexibility allows them to innovate, disrupt the market, and respond to new trends or threats more effectively than rigid competitors.

Example:

Apple initially focused on computers but pivoted into consumer electronics, launching the iPod, iPhone, and iPad, which transformed it into one of the world's most valuable companies. The company's ability to shift focus based on market opportunities gave it a significant competitive advantage. Moreover, as its customer base aged, it evolved its products and sales programs to create a direct-to-consumer business that was equally attractive to baby boomers, millennials, and newer generations.

Adapting strategies in response to changing conditions helps future-proof a business, ensuring it remains viable in the face of unpredictable disruptions, such as technological innovations or regulatory changes.

Example:

Netflix pivoted from DVD rentals to streaming services and later to content creation (original series like *Stranger Things*). Netflix also expanded its sources of content after testing and learning that U.S. customers are as open to programs from other countries (e.g., Spain, Korea) as the international Netflix audience is open to U.S.-created content. This gave the company access to a wide variety of new content at a more moderate cost, and this adaptability has allowed Netflix to stay ahead of competitors and secure a leading position in entertainment.

While a strong focus is always valuable in a business, being unreceptive to market and other changes is not conducive to long-term business growth and success. When things are not going well, it is important for leadership to ask the following questions:

a. Is this a temporary impediment that requires you to dig deeper and work harder to overcome the challenges?

b. Is the strategy correct, but the execution flawed, necessitating tweaks or significant changes to the implementation plan (and/or team)?

c. Is the strategy no longer relevant or viable, driving the need for a significant pivot and new direction?

The ability to pivot is a critical factor in helping a business SOAR. While some may view a pivot as a lack of focus or commitment to a strategy, it is, in fact, a powerful demonstration of resilience, innovation, and adaptability. Pivoting reflects a company's willingness to evolve and align with shifting market dynamics. The most successful businesses constantly reassess and refine their strategies, ensuring they stay relevant and competitive in an ever-changing landscape.

Markets are constantly evolving due to technological advancements, shifts in consumer preferences, regulatory changes, economic fluctuations, and competitive innovation. Businesses that fail to adapt risk irrelevance and, ultimately, obsolescence.

Conclusion

In an ever-changing business landscape, the ability to pivot is not just a strategy—it is a survival skill. Businesses that embrace adaptability and create a strong basic financial structure are well-placed to navigate challenges, seize new Opportunities, and maintain their relevance in dynamic markets. Choosing to pivot is not a sign of weakness or lack of focus; rather, it is a testament to resilience, strategic agility, and a commitment to long-term success.

Regular evaluation of strategies, execution, and outcomes is vital to ensuring that a business remains on course, even when external factors disrupt the status quo. By fostering a culture of innovation and adaptability, companies can position themselves to thrive in uncertainty, outpace competitors, and build enduring value. Pivoting is not about abandoning goals—it is about finding smarter, more effective paths to achieving them. When businesses remain open to change, they empower themselves to SOAR in the face of any challenge.

Chapter 19
Time to SOAR!

Doing business in today's world is not easy, especially for small and medium-sized businesses.

- Competition is intense and likely to remain so.
- New technologies, mega companies, and marketplaces threaten the business models of many smaller companies and have changed the landscape and delivery mechanism for many industries.
- Marketing and customer acquisition costs and methods have changed, frequently putting smaller companies at a disadvantage.
- Automation has facilitated huge strides in productivity for businesses that can fund the large, up-front costs for equipment, robotics, software, and related technology.
- Hiring and retaining the right talent is challenging in all fields—retail, services, manufacturing, and distribution.
- Changes and disruptions in supply chains continue to be part of the macro environment.
- Inflation and fluctuating costs have added to the complexity of running a business and pricing goods and services.

- Similarly, interest costs for borrowed money have fluctuated, putting strains on cash flow and profitability.
- Securing financing in volatile markets can be difficult.
- Cybersecurity is a constant threat, challenge, and cost for most businesses.
- External forces, including climate change, pandemics, political unrest, recessions, and wars, add challenges and complexities.
- Employees are expecting more, including work-life balance, flexible schedules, the ability to work from home, and opportunities for advancement.
- Artificial Intelligence presents potential risks and opportunities for many businesses.
- Customers have access to more choices and also face increasing demands and expectations from their suppliers.

Growth Is Very Attainable

Despite these challenges, growth is still very attainable for most businesses. The path forward, however, requires digging deeper, leveraging smarter tools, and adopting more structured methodologies to navigate complexity and seize opportunities to identify optimal paths to growth.

If you've already found your path to growth, we salute you and admire your success!

If you are still searching for a way forward, the SOAR process can help. With SOAR, you don't just get tools—you get an entire system and operating philosophy for identifying, prioritizing, and executing high-impact strategies tailored to your business.

So - Unlock Your Growth Potential and SOAR!

Our Companion to SOAR: SOARgrowth

After many years of developing and then applying the SOAR principles to companies we managed or advised, we identified a critical "unmet" need for small and medium-sized businesses: a simple, cost-effective way to access the growth knowledge and strategies available to larger organizations. To address this gap, we decided to "eat our own cooking." As a result, we developed SOARgrowth™, your personal business growth tool, process, resource, coach, and community—available at your fingertips at a fraction of the cost and time of any comparable alternative. SOARgrowth (SOARgrowth. com) offers a cost-effective, structured, and empowering platform to unlock your growth potential.

In a few hours, the SOARgrowth process empowers you and your team to streamline more than seven hundred potential growth Opportunities in the five to 15 most impactful strategies tailored to your business. Our combination of proprietary software built on the SOAR principles and a dedicated Growth Coach empower your team with sophisticated growth tools, insights, and support, making high-impact growth accessible without the high price tag or disruption of traditional consulting. Businesses can access actionable, data-driven growth strategies that were previously only available to large corporations with big budgets. Now, small and medium businesses can grow faster, make smarter decisions, and tap into expertise that builds long-term profitability and success.

How It Works

Our software leverages a powerful, streamlined survey system, engaging your management and senior team members to rank and prioritize potential growth opportunities suggested by the SOARgrowth platform. By focusing your team's expertise on what matters most, our platform highlights the best strategies for revenue and profitability growth—strategies tailored to your unique business landscape.

For the many businesses, especially small- and medium-sized ones, that lack the financial resources and time to access advanced business growth advice, SOARgrowth offers the capabilities of a top-tier strategy team in an accessible, easy-to-use online platform, putting advanced strategic insights at your fingertips and providing powerful guidance typically reserved for larger companies.

Key Features

- **Affordable, High-Impact Solutions:** Our platform delivers top-tier growth tools at a budget-friendly price, making it ideal for businesses that need strategic expertise without overextending on costs.

- **Strategic Prioritization Made Simple:** Our intuitive software does the heavy lifting by guiding your team through prioritizing the most impactful growth strategies. This simplifies decision-making and saves time, allowing your team to rapidly begin implementation of your best growth opportunities.

- **Expert Guidance at Your Fingertips:** SOARgrowth sets you up with a Growth Coach to assist you with optimizing the software, facilitate your team's working sessions, and to help you unlock the platform's full potential. Our Growth coaches don't just help you use the software—they bring years of growth strategy experience to your team, offering insights and guidance tailored to your specific business context.

- **Implementation Tools and Support:** Beyond strategy, we offer a suite of implementation tools and resources, ensuring that prioritized opportunities transition seamlessly from planning to action. Our support team and coaches work with you every step of the way to remove barriers and provide the resources needed to execute effectively.

Your Growth Spark Starts Here

SOARgrowth is more than a tool—it's a catalyst. It empowers businesses to overcome challenges, stimulate growth, and achieve their potential in today's competitive environment. If you're ready to transform your business and uncover new opportunities, SOARgrowth provides the roadmap, resources, and support to get you there.

Let's discover your "spark" for growth!

Learn more and begin your growth journey at SOARgrowth.com**.**

About the Authors

Larry Goddard

Whether serving as CEO, consultant, coach, or interim executive, Larry has helped more than three hundred middle-market and family businesses improve their growth, performance, profitability, financial strength, and value.

In addition to *SOAR to Business Success,* Larry has written three books on improving business performance, growth, profitability, and value. As the CEO of a national manufacturer and distributor of construction equipment and supplies, he grew revenues from $3 million to more than $100 million in eight years. Larry has extensive consulting, turnaround and advisory experience, including work as a supervisor with Price Waterhouse (Canada) and as a partner and management consulting practice leader at BDO USA LLP. He is currently the CEO of The Parkland Group, Inc., a strategy and growth consulting and coaching firm based in Cleveland, Ohio.

Larry is a chartered accountant (Canada-Inactive), chartered business valuator (Inactive), and certified turnaround professional. He serves on several private company advisory boards and has served on the board of directors of multiple private and publicly traded companies.

Laurence Franklin

Laurence has 40-plus years of experience establishing internationally renowned businesses and developing leading global brands. He specializes in developing and executing strategic growth plans and coaching executive teams.

After ten years working in accounting, transaction services, leverage buyouts, and management consulting, Laurence joined Tumi Inc. in 1985, establishing its premium positioning and overseeing revenue growth from $4M to approximately $55M. He then went on to join Coach as president, doubling sales to $550M+ and developing the company as a global lifestyle brand. Laurence held executive positions with Unilever as the EVP and GM of the Elizabeth Arden division.

In 2000, he returned to Tumi Inc., guiding the company through two private equity transactions in 2002 and 2004, and continued as CEO through 2009 and as a board member through 2011, with global revenues now in excess of $450 million. Soon afterward, Laurence joined Frette as CEO to position that business for new investors, departing in 2014 to serve as an advisor to high-

potential brands. Board memberships have included Rosetta Stone (NYSE), Travelpro, Human Touch, Buster + Punch, Fender Musical Instruments, and Made By Gather.

Once nationally ranked in the top ten in squash racquets, he still enjoys the occasional game with friends and his children. He resides in Los Angeles, California, and Milan, Italy.

Jennifer Goddard

Jennifer has over 25 years of sales and marketing experience with major consumer-facing brands and wholesale and retail organizations. She specializes in sales growth strategies, provides sales training, and acts as an interim sales executive and executive coach. Her expertise extends to product development, including licensed products, having worked with leading brands like Disney, Warner Brothers, Coca-Cola, Nabisco, and Bluey.

Jennifer has many years of experience as a sales and category manager selling to most of the major big box retailer chains in the United States and Canada, including grocery/drug, hardware/home center, and craft. She has also worked with traditional department and specialty store retailers.

Jennifer is a seasoned sales and executive coach dedicated to helping businesses, including family-run organizations, achieve sustained sales growth. Using her experience, she finds creative ways to drive sales growth, whether by leveraging licensing strategies to drive an increase in sales of over 40% in a single year, recruiting a national sales force of 84 people to drive an 85% sales increase in under six months, or developing a channel strategy to penetrate new customers, displace competitors' products, and establish category leadership to significantly increase sales.

She is currently the president of The Parkland Group, Inc., a strategy and growth consulting and coaching firm based in Cleveland, Ohio.

Thank You for Reading Our Book!

Just to say thanks for buying and reading our book,
we would like to give you a free SOARgrowth
welcome gift, no strings attached!

Scan the QR Code Here:

*We appreciate your interest in our book and value your
feedback as it helps us improve future versions.
We would appreciate it if you could leave your invaluable
review on Amazon.com with your feedback.*

www.ingramcontent.com/pod-product-compliance
Lightning Source LLC
Chambersburg PA
CBHW060615200326
41521CB00007B/779